nitty gritty books

- Chicken Cookbook
- Skillet Cookery
- Convection Oven
- Household Hints
- Seafood Cookbook
- Quick Breads
- Pasta & Rice
- Calorie Watchers Cookbook
- Pies & Cakes
- Yogurt
- The Ground Beef Cookbook
- Cocktails & Hors d'Oeuvres
- Casseroles & Salads
- Pressure Cooking
- Food Processor Cookbook

- Soups & Stews
- Crepes & Omelets
- Microwave Cooking
- Vegetable Cookbook
- Kid's Arts and Crafts
- Bread Baking
- The Crockery Pot Cookbook
- Classic Greek Cooking
- Low Carbohydrate Cookbook
- Kid's Cookbook
- Italian
- Cheese Guide & Cookbook
- Miller's German
- Quiche & Souffle

- To My Daughter With Love
- Natural Foods
- Chinese Vegetarian
- The Jewish Cookbook
- Working Couples
- Mexican
- Sunday Breakfast
- Fisherman's Wharf Cookbook
- Barbecue Cookbook
- Ice Cream Cookbook
- Blender Cookbook
- The Wok, a Chinese Cookbook
- Japanese Country
- Fondue Cookbook

designed with giving in mind

"To my daughter, Jennifer Laura,
and to my parents, Stanislav Kamil Wolf
and Jitka Kocourova Wolf."

CHICKEN Cookbook

by Stanley Wolf

illustrated by Mike Nelson

©Copyright 1980
Nitty Gritty Productions
Concord, California

A Nitty Gritty Book*
Published by
Nitty Gritty Productions
P.O. Box 5457
Concord, California 94524

*Nitty Gritty Books-Trademark
Owned by Nitty Gritty Productions
Concord, California

Printed in the U.S.A.
by Mariposa Press
Concord, California   ISBN 0-911954-56-2
Edited by Maureen Reynolds   Library of Congress Catalog Card Number: 80-81190

TABLE OF CONTENTS

Introduction 1
Purchasing Guide 4
Storage, Freezing and Thawing 6
Nutritive Value of Chicken 8
How To Disjoint a Whole Chicken 9
Boning a Chicken Breast 12
Two Basic Cooking Techniques 16
Other Ways to Prepare Chicken 19
Marinating Chicken 20
Testing for Doneness 21
Roast Chicken 23
Barbecued Chicken 43
Casseroles 53
Soups 63
Stews 73
Chicken Breasts 85
Chicken with Wines and Spirits 95
Chicken Flavored with Spices 107
International Classics 117
Oriental Delicacies 127
Chicken Cooked with Fruit 137
Nuts and Seeds Accompany Chicken 147
Precooked and Leftover Chicken ... 157
Chicken Parts 171
Index 180

INTRODUCTION

Present day chickens are descended from the jungle of Southeast Asia and appear to have been domesticated as early as 2500 B.C. However, until recent times, they remained an infrequent luxury at the dinner table. It used to take months to raise a bird to maturity, and hens were prized for their egg producing capability. As a result, the chickens which were picked for consumption were either stringy roasters or tough, old hens. Tender, young fowl were rarely available, and considered a special delicacy.

Today, of course, the situation has dramatically improved. Chicken is widely available and at very reasonable prices. Tender, young birds, (known as broilers or fryers) are no longer a rarity. Instead they are the variety which is most commonly marketed. This rapid change in the availability and quality of chickens has been due to the ingenuity of American poultry farmers and agricultural researchers. They worked to develop special breeding and nourishing techniques for producing plump and juicy chickens. They perfected methods which reduced the time required to mature the birds from months, to just weeks. Finally, they promoted efficient processing procedures and the use of rapid, refrigerated transportation to insure the delivery of fresh poultry to market. Thanks to this progress, chickens are now enjoyed regularly as a part of our diet.

Chicken is one of our favorite foods. We Americans enjoy its taste, appreciate its economy, and rely on its nutritional value. But the fact that chicken is also an extraordinarily versatile food is not as well recognized. Few cooks are aware that chicken is capable of being prepared in a greater number of ways than any other type of meat or fish. All too often, family chicken dinners are limited to fried chicken, or some type of chicken stew. Unfortunately, if a dish is served too frequently, some of its appeal is apt to be lost. Thus, the low-cost and nutritional benefits of chicken are not fully realized.

The inspiration for writing this book sprang from a desire to present a collection of recipes which would focus on the special versatility of chicken. The idea was to provide a source containing a wide variety of new and interesting ways to prepare chicken. It was hoped that many cooks would use it to learn to prepare and serve this economical and popular fowl more regularly. With this goal in mind, the book has been organized in the following manner: Some chapters include recipes in which only a specific cooking technique is utilized, such as roasting or barbecuing. Other chapters are dedicated to a particular category of ingredients with which chicken can be prepared, fruits, nuts, and spirits are some examples. Finally, some chapters are reserved for collections of more exotic recipes; these include international and oriental classics. Most traditional favorites have also been presented. Readers will also notice that recipes have been picked with an eye toward ease of preparation and minimum cooking time. Thus, the busy cook will discover many selections that are delicious, yet quick and easy to prepare. More elaborate meals, for company or that special occasion have not been neglected. There are many choices which will certainly dazzle even the most discriminating of food-lovers. All in all, it is hoped that the book will provide creative cooks with a vehicle for uncovering new and delightful chicken surprises.

PURCHASING GUIDE

The most reliable rule for purchasing chicken is: the fresher the better. However, freshly killed chickens are usually difficult, if not impossible to obtain. One should at least try to select poultry which has never been frozen. If you do find it necessary to purchase frozen poultry, inspect it thoroughly for signs of freezer burn or evidence of having been refrozen. If there is pinkish-colored ice in the package, it is a sign that the chicken has been at least partially defrosted and refrozen. Don't buy such a chicken. It will be tough and lacking in flavor.

Chickens are marketed under several different names, depending upon their age and weight. The following are the most commonly used classifications:

Broilers and Fryers: weigh from 2 to 4 pounds and are from 7 to 9 weeks old. They are bred for maximum tenderness. Broilers and fryers can be cooked in a wide variety of ways. They can be sauteed, roasted, broiled, fried or grilled.

Roasting Chickens: weigh from 3 to 5 pounds. They are slightly older than broilers and fryers, therefore a little less tender.

Capons: weigh from 4 to 8 pounds. They are roosters which have been castrated to improve their flavor and plumpness. Although they are somewhat older than roasting chickens, they are more tender.

Stewing Chickens: weigh from 4 to 7 pounds. They are the oldest of the four main types of chickens described here. Their flesh is tough and stringy, but rich in flavor. They are suitable for stewing only.

Chicken Parts: can be purchased separately. Packages of legs, thighs, breasts (boned and unboned), wings and backs can be found at your local market.

Chicken Giblets: which include the gizzard, heart and liver of the chicken can be found either inside a whole chicken or packaged separately. They are good sauteed and chopped up in stuffing, or prepared separately.

AN IMPORTANT FACT TO REMEMBER: It is much less expensive to buy a whole chicken and disjoint it yourself, than it is to buy separately packaged chicken parts. (To disjoint, see page 9.)

STORAGE, FREEZING AND THAWING

Chicken can be stored in the refrigerator or freezer according to the following guidelines:

Refrigerator Shelf:
Raw: Should be kept no longer than 2 days. Make sure to keep it well covered with plastic wrap to prevent drying out, but loose enough for air to circulate around chicken.
Cooked: Will keep well for no longer than a week. Make sure to keep it well covered.

Refrigerator Freezing Department:
    Raw: Will keep for up to 2 months, if packaged in an airtight container, or tightly wrapped and sealed in freezer paper.

    Cooked: Will keep for 2 weeks, if packaged in an airtight container, plastic wrap or freezer paper.

Freezer (0°F.):
    Raw: Will keep for up to 6 months, if packaged in an airtight container or freezer paper.

    Cooked: Will keep for up to 1 month, if packaged in an airtight container.

Once a chicken is defrosted, do not refreeze it. Use it within 2 days of thawing. If the thawing is done on a refrigerator shelf, allow 3 to 4 hours thawing time per pound. For example, a 2 to 3 pound broiler/fryer should thaw in 8 to 12 hours. To thaw more rapidly, place wrapped chicken in a pan under running water. Allow 1/2 to

1 hour per pound for broiler/fryers using this method. A microwave oven can thaw a frozen bird even more rapidly. Follow the microwave instructions. To guarantee even cooking throughout, make sure a chicken is thoroughly defrosted prior to cooking.

NUTRITIVE VALUE

Chicken is an excellent source of high-quality protein, a fine source of niacin, riboflavin, calcium, vitamin A and minerals. It is lower in fat and calories than most other meats. Because it is a short-fibered meat, it is also easy to digest.

LIGHT MEAT 3-1/2 ounces, without skin, cooked = 166 calories

DARK MEAT 3-1/2 ounces, without skin, cooked = 176 calories

HOW TO DISJOINT A WHOLE CHICKEN

Whole birds, pound for pound, are less expensive than chicken already cut into pieces. By learning how to cut chicken into pieces, you not only save money, but may end up with neater looking portions. It's really quite easy if you possess a sharp knife, a cutting board and a familiarity with the technique. For step-by-step instruction, with drawings, read the following:

1. TO REMOVE LEGS:
Place chicken on its back on a cutting board. Pull one leg away from the body and cut through the skin all the way down to the joint. Lift the chicken and bend the leg back until the thighbone is separated from the body. Repeat on other leg.

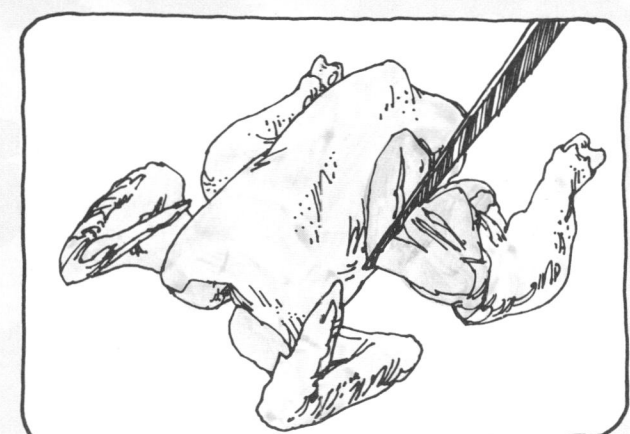

2. TO DIVIDE LEGS FROM THIGHS:
Grasp the drumstick in one hand and the thigh in the other. By bending the leg and thigh together, towards the center and the joint, you'll be able to locate the knee joint. Cut through this joint.

3. TO REMOVE WING FROM BODY:
Locate wing joint by rotating wing slightly. Cut on the inside of the wing, through the joint. Remove as little of the breast meat as possible. Repeat with other wing.

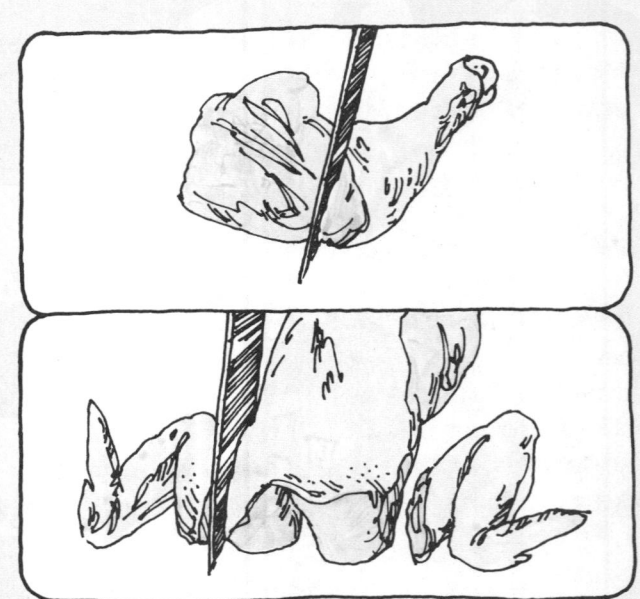

4. DIVIDING BREAST AND BACK:
Stand chicken on its neck and cut down along the breast end of the rib bones on each side. Separate the breast and back. Divide back into two pieces by breaking it at the joint and cutting through.

5. TO HALVE BREAST:
Place breast on cutting board, skin side up. Cut down along entire length of breastbone to separate breast into two halves.

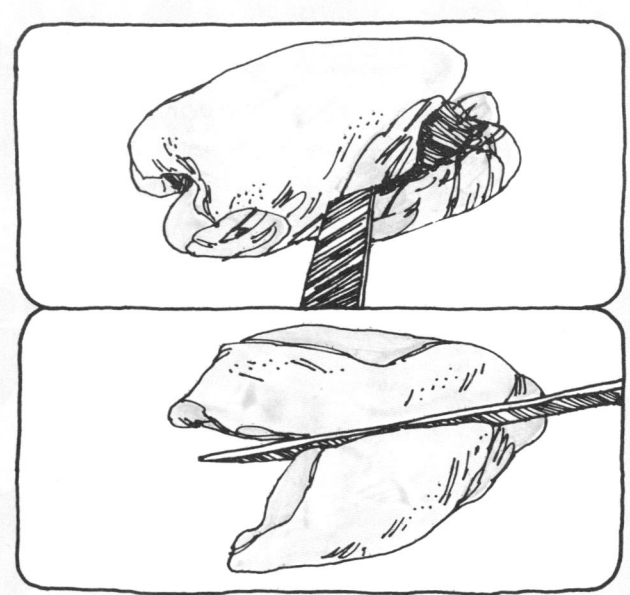

BONING A CHICKEN BREAST

Boning chicken breasts yourself serves two useful purposes. First, if chicken breasts are purchased already boned, they will have begun to lose some of their moisture and delightful flavor. Boning just prior to cooking helps to create a more delicious dish. Second, already boned breasts are relatively expensive. However, by boning breasts at home, chicken breast recipes become quite economical.

By the way, a chicken has only a single breast. That is, the entire portion of the chest, from the neck to the belly, is known as the breast of the chicken (including the skin, flesh and bones). The breast is usually halved after boning. Each half contains two filets, one slightly larger than the other. A boned, skinless breast half is also known as a supreme. The supreme is considered to be the finest part of the bird. If you have had the good fortune to savor perfectly prepared supremes, you will wholeheartedly agree.

How To Debone a Chicken Breast

1. Remove the skin from the breast by grasping the skin firmly in one hand and the flesh and bone in the other. Pull firmly to separate.

2. Place breast, skinned side down on a cutting board. Slit the thin membrane that covers the breastbone.

3. Grasp the breast and bend the breastbone at the wide end to separate it from the collarbones.

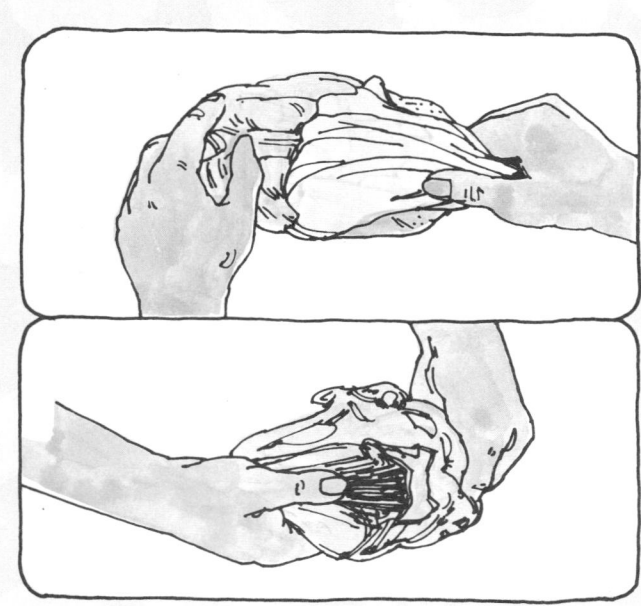

4. Twist the breastbone at the narrow end of the breast to separate it from the cartilage.

5. Gently pry out breastbone. Remove ribs by lifting them with your fingers.

6. Cut away cartilage from narrow end of breast. Carefully remove collarbones using the tip of a knife to cut through the flesh.

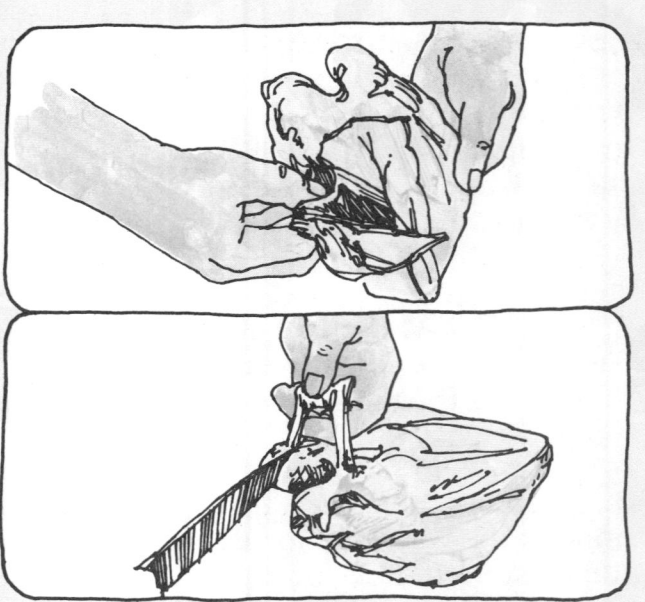

7. Using the tip of a knife, make a small incision along the length of the wishbone. Work the bone free with your fingers. Pull it out. It may be necessary to cut the flesh from the ends of the wishbone to take it out.

8. Cut the breast in half lengthwise to yield two supremes.

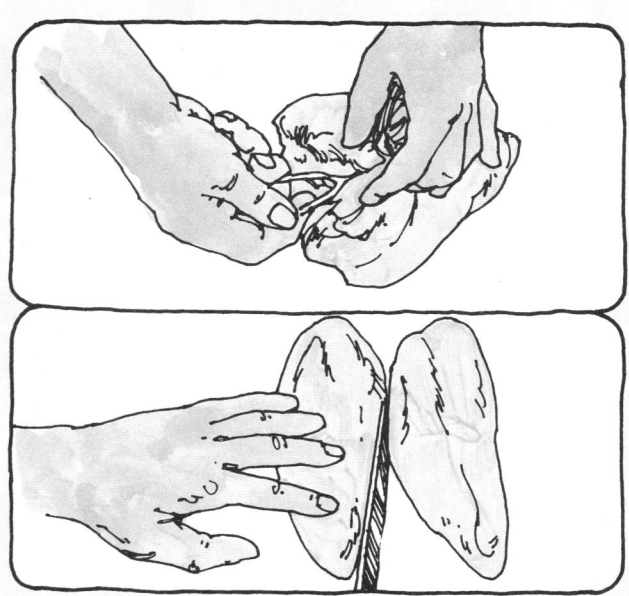

TWO BASIC COOKING TECHNIQUES

Two of the most basic and useful methods of cooking chicken are sauteeing and braising. Many recipes call for one or the other as a preliminary step. Familiarize yourself with each of these methods, and cooking chicken will become a lot simpler.

Sauteeing: is a method of pan frying chicken which uses just enough fat to keep the flesh from adhering to the bottom of the skillet. The chicken pieces are cooked over high heat, so that the surface of the chicken will become seared and golden brown. Sauteeing works particularly well for young broiler and fryer chickens that have been cut into pieces.

A lot of recipes call for sauteeing chicken just until it's brown. To do this, follow How to Saute Chicken, step 1. If you want to completely cook your chicken, follow How to Saute Chicken, steps 1 and 2.

How to Saute Chicken
Step 1: Pat chicken pieces dry with a paper towel. It's important to remove any surface moisture, because it will inhibit the browning process. Place a small amount of fat in a skillet (about 2 tablespoons for a 10-inch skillet), and heat it to a high

temperature. Place chicken pieces in skillet. Cook chicken until golden brown on all sides. Use tongs to turn chicken pieces. Never use a fork, or a sharp instrument to turn chicken pieces, they pierce the flesh and cause the juices which keep the chicken moist to escape. It will take about 6 minutes for the chicken to become golden brown.

Step 2: Follow step 1. Reduce the heat to medium-low and cover the skillet. Continue cooking the chicken, about 15 minutes for white meat and 20 minutes for dark meat. Turn pieces occasionally with tongs during cooking process.

Braising: is a method of cooking chicken in which the chicken (whole or in pieces) is first sauteed until brown (follow step 1 of How to Saute Chicken). Then simmered until done in a liquid that partially covers it. Cooking may take place in a skillet or a casserole. Vegetable, herbs and spices and generally added to the liquid in which the chicken cooks. Fats rise to the top of the skillet or casserole as the chicken cooks. They should be skimmed off and discarded before serving.

Braising can be successfully applied to the cooking of broilers and fryers, as well

as more mature birds, such as roasting chickens, capons and stewing chickens. Remember to allow more cooking time for the older birds.

When the liquid of a braised chicken dish is enriched at the end of the cooking time by the addition of eggs and cream, the result is known as a fricassee.

Other Ways to Prepare Chicken

Barbecuing and Broiling — are methods in which radiant heat is used to cook chicken quickly. When chicken is barbecued or broiled, the most moist and delicious results are achieved if intense heat causes the outside of the chicken to become browned and crisp, which allows the natural juices of the chicken to remain sealed in. See the chapter entitled **Barbecued** for more details (page 44).

Roast — chicken is cooked in an oven until the skin is richly browned and the meat is succulent and juicy. The seven steps to perfectly roasted chicken are outlined in the chapter entitled **Roast Chicken** (see page 24).

Frying — is a method in which chicken is cooked in oil or fat, in a skillet. There are two types of frying: pan frying, which uses small amounts of oil; and deep-fat frying, which uses large amounts of oil. The trick with both of these methods, is to keep the oil hot enough to cook the chicken without burning it. To insure that the oil stays hot, don't crowd the pan. If the oil isn't hot enough, the chicken will become greasy and take longer to cook. For more details about these types of cooking see Deep Fried Chicken and Maryland Fried Chicken, pages 124 and 125 respectively.

MARINATING A CHICKEN

Marinating chicken adds a whole new dimension to its flavor. Subtle combinations of liquids, herbs and spices penetrate the flesh and produce exceptionally tender and juicy chicken. Acidic liquids, such as lemon juice, wine and vinegar, break down the muscle tissue of the chicken, making it more tender. Oils work to seal in the juices. Chicken is often marinated prior to broiling, barbecuing, sauteeing or deep-fat frying.

To Marinate: immerse the chicken completely in the marinade. Not only will the marinade work faster, but the chicken will be more flavorful too. There are two ways of marinating chicken. You may let it stand from two to four hours at room temperature, or you may place it in the refrigerator for 24 to 48 hours. If you choose the latter method, be sure to turn the chicken twice daily. The reason for this is that the acidic liquids have a tendency to remain at the bottom. If you don't turn the chicken, it may assume a very tart and acidic flavor. After the chicken is finished marinating, dry it well with paper towels before you cook it. Leftover marinade may be used to baste the chicken while it cooks.

TESTING FOR DONENESS

Although many rule-of-thumb techniques are used to determine if a chicken has been sufficiently cooked, the only reliable and accurate method requires the insertion of an instant-registering meat thermometer into the meat. Insert the thermometer into the center of the inner thigh muscle, taking care not to make contact with the bone. Dark chicken meat is done when the internal temperature reads 180°F. and white meat is cooked when the thermometer reaches 145°F. The center of a stuffed bird should reach at least 165°F.

Other methods, such as piercing the flesh deeply and noting the color of the running juices, wiggling the drumstick, or pressing the surface and observing the resilience of the meat, are all much less dependable. It is much better to purchase an instant-registering meat thermometer and use it whenever cooking a chicken. The technique is equally accurate for all methods of cooking chicken.

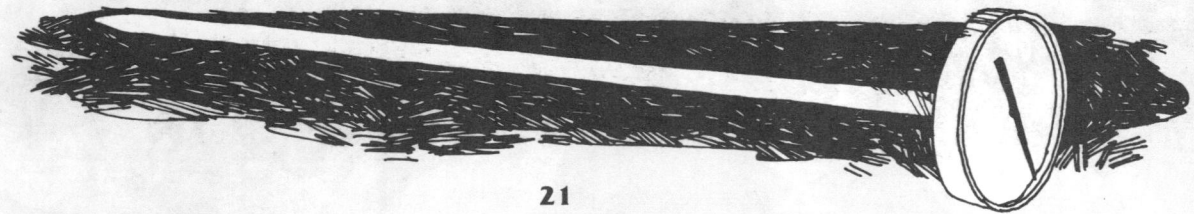

ROAST CHICKEN

Introduction 24
Roasting Chicken Timetable 26
How to Truss a Chicken 28
How to Carve a Roast Chicken 30
Roast Chicken
    Master Recipe (Unstuffed) 32
Flavored Butters 34
Roasting a Stuffed Chicken
    (Master Recipe) 36
Chicken Stuffings
    Simple Grape Stuffing 37
    Simple Bread Stuffing 37
    Bread, Nut, and Apple Stuffing . . 37
    Cranberry-Orange Stuffing 38
    Brandied-Pecan Stuffing 39
Spit-Roasted Chicken 40
Chicken Roasted in Salt 41

Preparing a beautifully roasted chicken does require a bit of patience and care. However, it is not a complex task and the finished product is well worth the effort. Unfortunately, overcooking and underattention usually prevent a perfectly cooked bird, with crisp, brown skin and succulent, tender flesh from reaching the table. Therefore, if one wants to roast chicken to perfection, the following sequence of steps must carefully be carried out: (1) Oiling or buttering the bird. (2) Properly filling it with stuffing (if desired). (3) Trussing the chicken. (4) Using a rack. (5) Roasting at the temperature and time recommended in the Roasting Timetable on page 26. (6) Sealing (this action is performed by basting during roasting). (7) Turning. Here's a detailed description of each of these steps.

(1) **Oiling or Buttering** the bird helps seal in the juices while it's cooking and also adds a fine flavor. Various flavors can be added and used to modify the basic roast chicken taste. Flavored butter recipes are given on pages 34 and 35.
(2) **Stuffings** provide additional variations on the theme of the basic roast chicken. In the master recipe for Roasting a Stuffed Chicken (page 36) some guidelines are

presented for preparing a stuffed bird. Several delicious stuffing recipes are also suggested (see pages 37, 38 and 39).

(3) **Trussing** is a method of tying a chicken so that it maintains its shape while roasting. The chicken is thus more attractive when finally ready to serve. It is also easier to carve and handle. A simple method for trussing a chicken is shown on page 28.

(4) **Using a Rack** allows heat to circulate evenly around the chicken while cooking, thus surrounding it with dry heat. Without a rack, the bottom of the bird will stew and the upper portion will roast. To start roasting, place the chicken on its side on the rack. Turning the chicken during roasting is discussed in step 7.

(5) **A Roasting Timetable** giving estimated roasting times for various sized birds is found on page 26. The roasting temperature of 450°F. is probably higher than the roasting temperatures recommended in other cooking guides. Although lower temperatures may also be used, the 450°F. temperature gives unsurpassed results! The higher temperature will cause a little more spattering in the oven near the end of the roasting time, but the succulent results are worth it. If you would prefer to use a lower temperature, first set the oven at 450°F., put in the

chicken and immediately reduce the heat to 350°F. and roast for about 20 minutes per pound. Check for doneness with an instant-registering meat thermometer.

(6) **Sealing** a chicken is critical to good roasting. A one-way "screen" must be formed on the outside of the chicken which allows heat to enter, but keeps the juices from escaping. The butter or oil which is rubbed and basted onto the chicken prior to, and while roasting forms such a seal. This results in a more moist bird.

(7) **Turning** while roasting permits uniform browning and cooking of the chicken. By starting to roast the chicken while on its side and then turning periodically, the juices are also kept from collecting in a region of the bird near the legs and thighs. The chicken should be turned without piercing the skin. This can be done by inserting a fork into the neck cavity and turning the bird.

CHICKEN ROASTING TIMETABLE

CHICKEN WEIGHT (Ready to Cook)	OVEN TEMP.	COOKING TIME (Unstuffed)	COOKING TIME (Stuffed)
3/4 to 1 pound	450°F.	25 to 30 minutes	30 to 35 minutes
1-1/2 to 2 pounds	450°F.	35 to 40 minutes	40 to 50 minutes
2-1/2 to 3 pounds	450°F.	45 to 50 minutes	55 to 60 minutes
3-1/2 to 4 pounds	450°F.	50 to 60 minutes	65 to 75 minutes
4-1/2 to 5 pounds	450°F.	55 to 65 minutes	70 to 80 minutes
5-1/2 to 6 pounds	450°F.	65 to 75 minutes	75 to 85 minutes

HOW TO TRUSS A CHICKEN

(1) Start with a piece of clean string suitable for trussing, about 3 feet long. Place bird on its back, legs facing towards you. Tie the legs together tightly by looping the string around their ends. Try to keep the ends of string reasonably even in length. Cross the two ends of the string, pull the two ends around the tail in a loop and tighten the string. This will pull the tail up towards the legs. Bring the ends of the string along both sides of the chicken. Guide them under the drumsticks.

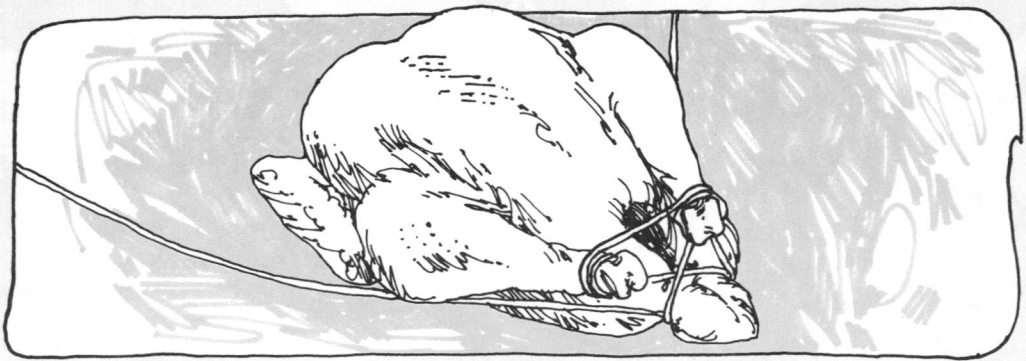

(2) Turn chicken on its breast. Thread string through the wings and pull together along a line across the chicken back. Make sure that string is taut. Tie securely with knot, cut off any excess string.

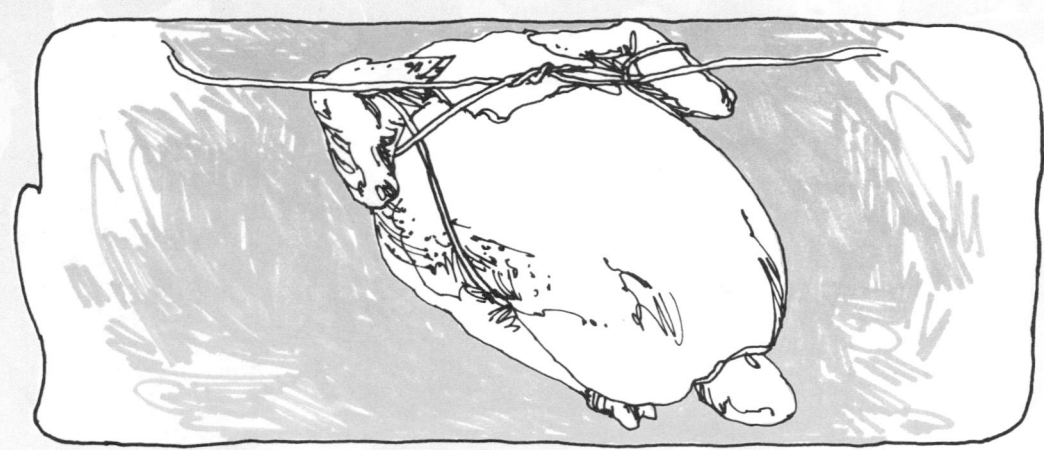

HOW TO CARVE A ROAST CHICKEN

Let chicken rest at room temperature for 15 minutes before carving. This allows the juices to settle into the flesh. Remove trussing strings.

(1) Place chicken breast side up. Insert fork into leg, gently pull leg while cutting skin all around. Pierce the joint that connects the leg and thigh to the carcass, and separate from the body. Do likewise with the other leg.

(2) Holding chicken with the fork through the breast, cut through the shoulder joint where the wing and the body are connected. Cut off as little breast meat as possible when removing the wing.
(3) To carve breast, hold chicken firmly in place by pressing fork into breastbone on the half that you are going to carve. Slice down diagonally through the meat. Lift off each slice as you cut it.

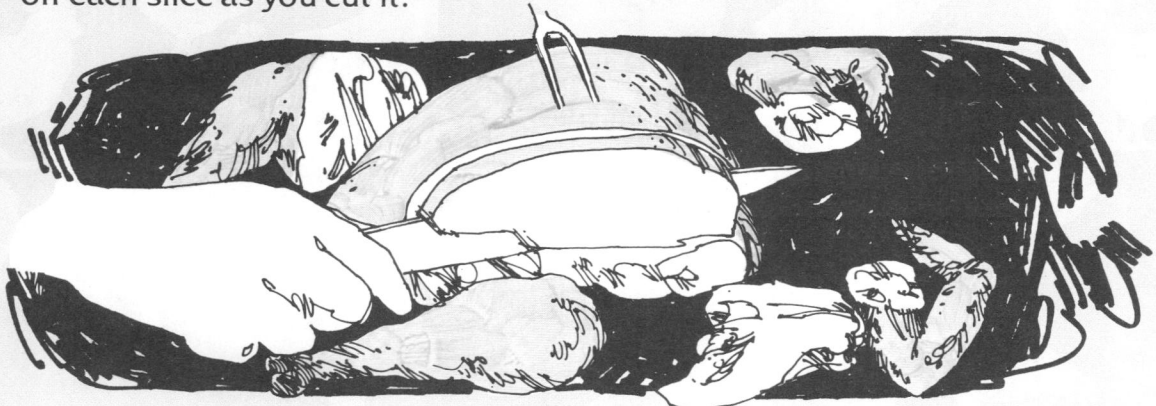

ROAST CHICKEN MASTER RECIPE (UNSTUFFED)

All you ever needed to know about how to roast a chicken, but were afraid to ask.

1 chicken, 2-1/2 to 3 lbs.
1/2 cup butter, flavored butter, or 1/3 cup oil
    (recipes for flavored butters given on pages 34 and 35)
freshly ground pepper
salt

Preheat oven to 450°F. Remove giblets and excess fat from chicken cavity. Rinse and remove excess moisture with paper towels. Rub cavity with salt and pepper and place 2 tablespoons butter within, or rub with oil. Dry outside of chicken thoroughly with paper towels. This will aid browning. Truss chicken as shown on page 28. Rub outside with 2 tablespoons butter or oil. Sprinkle salt and pepper on outside of bird. Place chicken on its **side** on rack in roasting pan. Rack allows even heat circulation around bird during roasting. Place pan with chicken in middle of heated oven. **Roast chicken at 450°F. for entire roasting time** (see chicken roasting timetable, page 24).

Melt remaining butter in skillet over medium heat. After 1/3 of total roasting time (15 minutes in this case), baste chicken with butter. Turn bird onto its other side without piercing skin. After 2/3 of time has elapsed, turn bird onto its back and baste with juices at bottom of roasting pan. When near end of cooking time, insert instant-registering meat thermometer into thickest part of thigh. When 170ºF. is registered, chicken is perfectly cooked. Remove bird from oven and let rest 10 minutes before carving. This allows juices to settle into flesh. The rich pan drippings are all the sauce that is needed. Remove trussing strings before carving. Makes 4 servings.

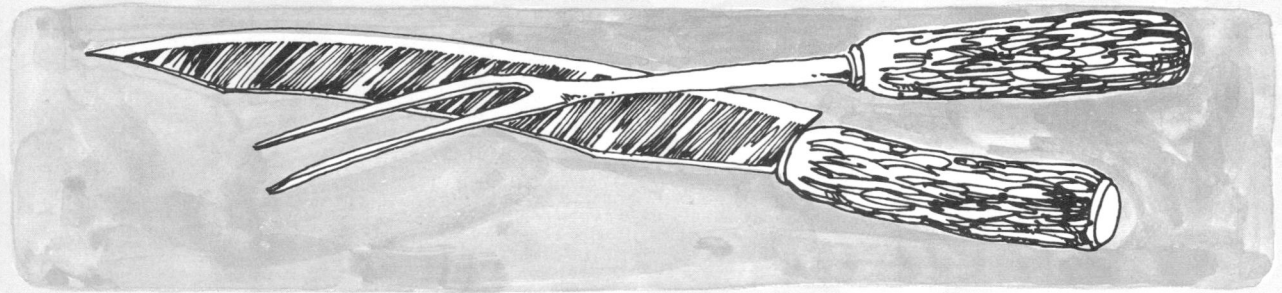

FLAVORED BUTTERS

For additional interest, flavored butter can be used in place of plain butter to heighten the flavor of basic roast chicken. To make flavored butter, always start with cold butter. It will become fluffy when beaten. Warm butter, on the other hand, will become oily and slick. Spices and herbs other than those suggested can also be used.

FLAVORED BUTTER MASTER RECIPE

1/2 cup cold butter
flavoring ingredients (any of the suggestions on page 35)

Beat butter until fluffy. Beat in additional ingredients. If unsalted butter is used, add 1 teaspoon salt. Omit if butter is salted. Refrigerate 10 to 15 minutes before use. Will flavor 1 to 2 chickens.

Prepare according to the directions for the Flavored Butter Master Recipe on the preceding page.

PARSLEY BUTTER

1/2 cup cold butter
1/2 cup fresh chopped parsley
1/4 tsp. freshly ground pepper

GARLIC BUTTER

1/2 cup cold butter
3 to 4 cloves of garlic, crushed
1/4 tsp. freshly ground pepper

LEMON-CURRY BUTTER

1/2 cup cold butter
1 to 2 tsp. curry powder
2 tsp. grated lemon rind
1/4 tsp. freshly ground pepper

GINGER BUTTER

1/2 cup cold butter
1 tbs. ground ginger
1/4 tsp. ground cinnamon
1 garlic clove, crushed
1 tsp. soy sauce
1/4 tsp. freshly ground pepper

ROASTING A STUFFED CHICKEN

Here's a good, basic recipe for those who prefer their birds stuffed.

Stuffing, your choice (see pages 37 through 39)
1 chicken, 4-1/2 to 5 lbs.

4 tbs. butter
salt and pepper

Prepare stuffing according to desired recipe. Allow to return to room temperature. Loosely fill chicken cavity. Do not overstuff. Stuffing will expand as it absorbs juices during cooking. (Extra stuffing can be baked in separate pan.) Truss the chicken according to directions on page 28. Rub outside of chicken with 2 tablespoons of butter. Sprinkle with salt and pepper. Preheat oven 450°F. Place chicken on its side on rack in roasting pan, then into oven. Melt remaining butter. After 1/3 roasting time has elapsed, baste chicken with butter and turn over onto other side, being careful not to pierce skin. Roast for another 1/3 of total time. Baste with pan drippings and turn bird on its back. Roast for final 1/3 of cooking time. Test for doneness at end of cooking time with instant-registering thermometer (should register 170°F.). Remove from oven and let rest 10 minutes before carving.

SIMPLE GRAPE STUFFING

Merely fill the cavity of a chicken with washed and de-stemmed seedless, green grapes. While roasting, the grapes will absorb the chicken juices and taste marvelous.

SIMPLE BREAD STUFFING

1/4 cup butter
1/4 cup chopped onion
1/2 tsp. sage

1/4 tsp. salt
1/4 tsp. pepper

4 cups dry bread crumbs
1 cup chicken broth

Melt butter in saucepan over medium heat. Saute onions in butter until tender. Add sage, salt and pepper. Combine with bread crumbs. Add broth, tossing well. Produces enough stuffing for a 4-1/2 to 5 pound bird. Can be baked in covered casserole at 325°F. for 45 minutes.

Apple-Nut Stuffing Variation: saute 1/4 cup chopped celery with onion. Add 1 peeled, cored and chopped apple, 1/2 cup slivered almonds and 1/4 cup raisins to stuffing before filling chicken.

CRANBERRY-ORANGE STUFFING

A festive, autumn stuffing.

2/3 cup chopped fresh cranberries
2 tbs. sugar
2 tsp. grated orange peel
1/2 tsp. salt
1/4 tsp. ground cinnamon
3 cups dried raisin bread cubes
2 tbs. melted butter or margarine
1/4 cup orange juice

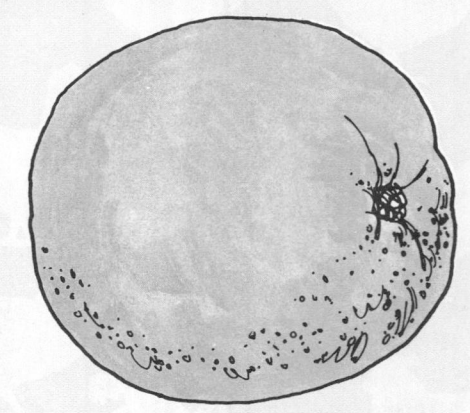

    Combine cranberries, sugar, orange peel, salt and cinnamon in bowl. Add bread cubes and drizzle with melted butter and orange juice. Stir lightly to mix. Produces enough stuffing for a 4-1/2 to 5 pound chicken. Can be baked in covered casserole at 325°F. for 45 minutes.

BRANDIED-PECAN STUFFING

A rich taste and nutty texture recommend this spirited stuffing.

1 cup apple juice
1/4 cup apricot or peach-flavored brandy
1/4 cup butter or margarine
1 pkg. (8 ozs.) corn bread stuffing mix
3/4 cup pecans

Combine juice, brandy and butter in saucepan. Place over medium heat. Stir until butter melts. Add stuffing mix and pecans, tossing lightly to blend. Produces enough stuffing for a 4-1/2 to 5 pound chicken. Can be baked in covered casserole at 325°F. for 45 minutes.

SPIT ROASTED CHICKEN

Spit roasting was probably one of the first ways of preparing chicken. Because it yields such marvelous results, the method still has enthusiastic adherents.

1 chicken, 2-1/2 to 3 lbs.
salt and pepper

4 tbs. butter, semi-soft
3 to 4 bacon strips

Rub salt and pepper inside chicken cavity. Place 2 tablespoons butter inside cavity. Truss chicken (see page 28). Rub outside of chicken with 2 tablespoons butter and sprinkle with salt and pepper. Push spit through chicken, starting at tail end. Blanch bacon strips in boiling water for 5 minutes. This removes smokey taste of bacon which would overwhelm flavor of chicken. Tie bacon strips over breast and thighs of chicken in an "X" pattern. No basting will be needed while roasting, due to bacon. Roast chicken over hot coals turning appropriately. Use roasting timetable for time estimate (see page 36). Fat should fall into drip pan placed under spit, not on coals. Fifteen minutes before chicken is done, remove bacon. Then allow chicken to brown uniformly. Check for doneness per instructions on page 21. Serve pan drippings as sauce. Makes 4 servings.

CHICKEN ROASTED IN SALT

Chicken roasted in salt is incomparably moist and tender. An ancient technique that deserves modern attention.

12 lbs. purified rock salt
1 chicken, 3-1/2 lbs.

Place 2 inches of salt in Dutch oven. Wash chicken. Set chicken breast side up onto salt while still wet. Cover both chicken cavities with foil to prevent salt crust from collapsing during roasting, as well as to keep salt from dissolving into meat. Cover chicken completely with salt, packing tightly. Cover Dutch oven tightly. Roast chicken at 400°F. for 1-1/2 hours. Test for doneness using instant-registering meat thermometer. Pick small hole in salt and insert thermometer into chicken. When thermometer registers 170°F., chicken is done. If necessary, fill hole with salt and continue roasting. When ready to serve, break away and discard salt. Remove any bits of salt clinging to chicken. Makes 4 servings.

BARBECUED CHICKEN

Introduction to Barbecuing
    and Broiling Chicken........... 44
Caraway Chicken Halves........... 46
Chicken Teriyaki.................. 47
Foil-Wrapped Barbecued Chicken.... 51
Grilled Island Chicken 48
Sweet and Sour Barbecued Chicken .. 49
Texas Barbecued Chicken 50

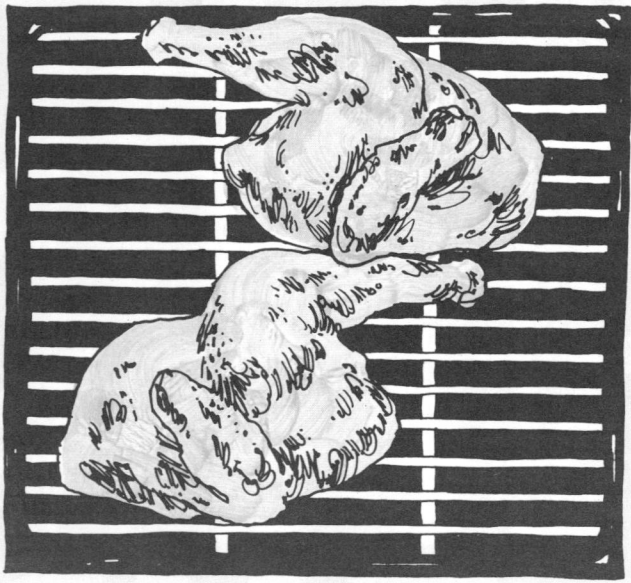

BARBECUING AND BROILING CHICKEN

Barbecuing (grilling) and broiling are both methods of cooking in which radiant heat is used to cook food quickly. When chicken is barbecued or broiled, the moistest and tastiest results are achieved if intense heat cause the outside of the chicken to become brown and crisp while allowing natural juices to remain sealed in. Contrary to common belief, it is this browning, together with the intensity of heat, that gives barbecued chicken its special flavor and character and not the taste of the charcoal.

To insure that the sealing and browning process occurs properly during barbecuing or broiling, the following procedures should be applied: The chicken joints should be broken so that the pieces will lay flat and all the meat will be at about the same distance from the heat source. If no marinade or barbecuing sauce is being used the chicken should be rubbed dry and then basted with a thin layer of oil before cooking. The oil will assist in creating a screen which seals in the natural juices, but allows the heat to enter and cook the meat. Basting during barbecuing continues to protect this seal. Next, the chicken pieces should be placed close enough to the heat source to permit the intense heat to seal and brown the meat, but just far enough away to avoid burning. Frequent monitoring and adjusting of the distance may be necessary, until a thorough familiarity with a given heat source is acquired. Ingredients in the barbecue or basting sauce may require further adjustment of the cooking distance. For example, honey or sugar based sauces can char more easily than others. When using a charcoal grill, chicken can usually be placed 2 to 3 inches from the coals, while in an oven broiler, the distance is more variable (3 to 6 inches) depending on the broiler design. Tongs rather than a fork should always be used for turning. The tongs will not pierce the skin and cause the seal to break.

If a **charcoal grill** is used, an even, intense heat source will be created by a full bed of charcoal briquettes which have burned until they become glowing coals covered with a layer of gray ash. If an oven broiler is used, pre-heat the broiler (but not the broiling pan) for 5 to 10 minutes.

Cooking time for chicken pieces on a charcoal grill is about 25 to 30 minutes per side. In an oven broiler, the chicken will cook in 15 to 20 minutes per side. Testing for doneness should be performed with an instant-registering meat thermometer. White meat is done when the thermometer registers 140°F. and dark meat is done at 165°F.

CARAWAY CHICKEN HALVES

To reach its full flavor potential, the chicken should marinate several hours at room temperature, or overnight in the refrigerator.

1/2 cup vegetable oil
1/4 cup light corn syrup
1/4 cup chopped onion
1 tbs. lemon juice
1 tsp. dried oregano
1 tsp. caraway seed
1/2 tsp. salt
2 chickens, 2 to 2-1/2 lbs. each, split in half, lenthwise

Combine oil, syrup, onion, lemon juice, oregano, caraway seed and salt in bowl. Mix well. Marinate chicken in mixture. Break joints and place chicken halves on grill, bone side down. Broil over **slow** coals 25 minutes. Turn, broil 20 minutes more, brushing occasionally with sauce. Continue broiling, 10 minutes more, or until meat is tender, turning occasionally and brushing with marinade. Makes 4 servings.

CHICKEN TERIYAKI

Teriyaki-style barbecuing originated in Japan.

1/2 cup soy sauce
1 clove garlic, minced
3 tbs. sugar
2 tbs. fresh ginger, minced
1/2 cup orange juice (fresh, if possible)
3 tbs. vegetable oil
1/4 cup sherry
1 chicken, 2-1/2 to 3 lbs. cut into serving pieces

Mix together soy sauce, garlic, sugar, ginger, orange juice, oil and sherry in bowl. Toss chicken in this mixture to coat well and marinate 1 to 2 hours at room temperature. Turn at least twice while marinating. Reserve marinade. Broil or barbecue for 15 minutes on each side. Remove chicken from heat and replace in marinade an for additional 30 minutes to absorb more flavor. Finish by barbecuing or broiling each piece 10 to 15 minutes more on each side. Makes 4 servings.

GRILLED ISLAND CHICKEN

A dish of Hawaiian inspiration. Perfect with rice and a fresh fruit salad.

1 can (8-3/4 ozs.) crushed pineapple
1 cup firmly packed brown sugar
2 tbs. lemon juice
2 tbs. mustard
2 chickens, 2-1/2 to 3 lbs. each, quartered
1/2 cup vegetable oil
salt and pepper

Drain pineapple, reserving 2 tablespoons syrup. Make glaze by combining pineapple, sugar, lemon juice, mustard and reserved syrup. Brush chicken quarters with oil and sprinkle with salt and pepper. Grill over medium-hot coals, skin side up for 30 minutes. Turn skin side down and grill 20 minutes more. Brush both sides of chicken with glaze. Broil another 10 minutes, brushing each side twice more with glaze. Heat extra glaze and serve as accompaniment. Makes 4 to 6 servings.

SWEET AND SOUR BARBECUED CHICKEN

In this recipe, chicken is first simmered in the barbecue sauce, then marinated to absorb more flavor. Finally, it is richly browned on a barbecue.

1/3 cup lemon juice	1/2 tsp. salt
1/3 cup honey	1/4 tsp. basil
2 tbs. Worcestershire Sauce	1/4 tsp. hot pepper sauce
3 tbs. mustard	1 chicken, 2-1/2 to 3 lbs,
1/2 cup white wine	cut into serving pieces

Combine lemon juice, honey, Worcestershire, mustard, wine, salt, basil and pepper sauce in Dutch oven. Bring to boil and add chicken pieces turning to cover with sauce. Reduce heat, cover, simmer for 35 minutes, until chicken is almost tender. Remove pot from heat and let stand 30 minutes to 3 hours at room temperature. When ready to barbecue, remove chicken from sauce and place on grill 4 to 6 inches from hot coals. Turn pieces often until browned and thoroughly heated through, basting frequently with sauce. Makes 4 servings.

TEXAS BARBECUED CHICKEN

A good all-purpose barbecue sauce. Try it on ribs too.

1/4 cup butter	1 tsp. mustard
1/4 cup molasses	1 tsp. salt
1 garlic clove, crushed	1/4 tsp. pepper
1/2 tsp. paprika	2 chickens, 2-1/2 to 3 lbs. each
2 tbs. tarragon vinegar	cut into halves
3/4 cup catsup	salt and pepper
1 tbs. Worcestershire sauce	chili powder

Combine butter, molasses, garlic, paprika, vinegar, catsup, Worcestershire, mustard, salt and pepper in saucepan. Simmer 20 minutes over low heat. Stir occasionally. Break chicken joints. Rub chicken with salt, pepper and chili powder. Place skin sides up, 3 inches from hot coals. Cook, about 30 minutes on each side. Baste with sauce often. Makes 4 to 6 servings.

FOIL-WRAPPED BARBECUED CHICKEN

An interesting variation on the usual barbecuing technique. The chicken pieces are super moist and tasty when prepared this way.

1/2 recipe of Texas Barbecue Chicken Sauce (see recipe page 50)
1 chicken, 2-1/2 to 3 lbs., cut into serving pieces

Prepare sauce according to directions. Dip chicken pieces into sauce. Place each piece on an 8-inch square layer of heavy duty aluminum. Pour 2 tablespoons sauce over each piece. Seal foil, leaving room for expansion of steam. Place on grill over hot coals. Cook 50 to 60 minutes. During last 15 minutes, open foil and brush with sauce. Makes 4 servings.

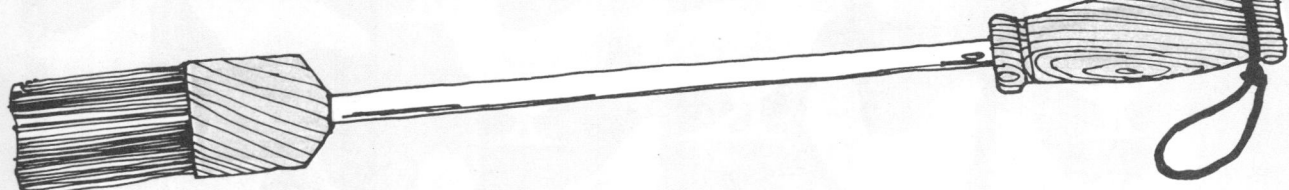

CHICKEN CASSEROLES

Almond Chicken Casserole 54
Chicken Hacienda 55
Chicken and Sauerkraut Casserole . . . 56
Chicken-Sweet Potato Pie 57
Creamy Baked Chicken 59
Popover Chicken-Tarragon Casserole 60
Easy Chicken Pot Pie 61

ALMOND CHICKEN CASSEROLE

This recipe is easy enough to prepare any day of the week. The real bonus is that it's also delicious enough to serve to your most special company.

1/2 cup sliced fresh mushrooms
1 tbs. butter
3 cups cooked rice
1 cup chicken broth
3 cups cubed cooked chicken
3/4 cup chopped celery
1 can (10-1/2 ozs.) cream of mushroom soup
1 cup sliced almonds

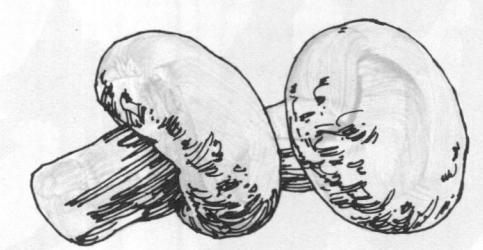

Saute mushrooms in butter just until limp. Combine mushrooms, rice, chicken broth, chicken, celery and soup. Pour into greased 1-quart casserole dish. Sprinkle with almonds. Bake at 325°F. for 45 minutes. Makes 4 to 6 servings.

CHICKEN HACIENDA

1/2 cup all-purpose flour
1 tsp. salt
1/2 tsp. pepper
1/2 tsp. paprika
1 chicken 2-1/2 to 3 lbs.,
 cut into serving pieces
2 tbs. vegetable oil
4 strips bacon

2 carrots, sliced
1 can (4 ozs.) chopped green chilies
1 tbs. chopped fresh parsley
1 bay leaf
1/2 tsp. thyme
1 lemon, thinly sliced
2 cups tomato juice

Combine flour, salt, pepper and paprika in bowl. Roll chicken pieces in seasoned flour. Pour oil into large skillet. Place over medium-high heat. Add chicken pieces and brown well on all sides. Remove chicken to large casserole dish. Lay bacon strips over chicken. Add carrots, chilies, parsley, bay leaf and thyme to casserole. Top with lemon slices and pour tomato juice over all. Cover and bake at 350°F. for 1 hour. Skim and discard fat before serving. Makes 4 servings.

CHICKEN AND SAUERKRAUT CASSEROLE

4 strips bacon
1/3 cup all-purpose flour
1/2 tsp. salt
1/8 tsp. pepper
1 chicken, 2-1/2 to 3 lbs., cut into serving pieces
1 cup chopped onion

1 clove garlic, crushed
1/2 tsp. thyme
2 tbs. all-purpose flour
1-1/2 cups chicken stock
1 can (16 ozs.) sauerkraut, drained
1 tbs. sugar

Fry bacon in skillet until crisp. Remove and drain on paper towels. Crumble bacon when cool. Reserve bacon drippings. Mix flour, salt and pepper together in bowl. Roll chicken in mixture. Place chicken in bacon drippings over medium-high heat. Brown pieces well on all sides. Remove chicken and set aside. Add onion, garlic and thyme to skillet. Saute until onion is tender. Blend in flour and cook 1 minute, stirring constantly. Gradually add chicken broth. Cook, stirring, until mixture thickens. Stir in bacon, sauerkraut and sugar. Bring to boil. Pour into 3-quart casserole dish. Cover with chicken pieces. Bake at 350°F. for 50 to 60 minutes. Skim and discard fat before serving. Makes 4 servings.

CHICKEN AND SWEET POTATO PIE

You'll be reminded of Thanksgiving when you sample this spicy dish. This is sure to be a "hit with pumpkin pie lovers.

2 cups mashed sweet potatoes
2 tbs. firmly packed brown sugar
1/4 tsp. salt
1/2 tsp. cinnamon
1/8 tsp. allspice
1/3 cup undiluted evaporated milk

2 tbs. butter
1/4 cup finely minced onions
1 can (5 ozs.) water chestnuts, quartered
1 can (10-1/2 ozs.) cream of chicken soup
3 cups cooked, diced chicken

Mix sweet potatoes, brown sugar, salt, cinnamon, allspice and milk together in bowl. Spread mixture in a ring in a greased 2-quart casserole dish. In a skillet, melt butter over medium heat. Saute onions and water chestnuts about 5 minutes, or until onions are translucent. Add soup, chicken and 2 tablespoons water. Heat, stirring occasionally. Pour into center of potato-ringed casserole. Bake at 400°F. for 20 to 30 minutes. Makes 6 servings.

CHICKEN-VEGETABLE CASSEROLE

The frozen orange juice concentrate adds a special tang to this tasty casserole.

1/2 cup all-purpose flour
1-1/2 tsp. salt
1/4 tsp. pepper
1 tbs. paprika
1 chicken, 2-1/2 to 3 lbs., cut into serving pieces
2 tbs. vegetable oil

1 can (8 ozs.) whole onions, drained
1/2 cup chopped carrots
1 can (8 ozs.) sliced mushrooms
1 tbs. sugar
1/3 cup frozen orange juice concentrate, thawed

Mix flour, salt, pepper and paprika together in bag. Shake chicken pieces, 2 at a time, in mixture. Reserve 2 tablespoons of leftover flour mixture. Heat oil over medium-high heat in large skillet. Add chicken and brown well on all sides. Remove chicken to baking dish together with onions, carrots and mushrooms. Add reserved flour and sugar to skillet, stirring until smooth paste is formed. Add juice concentrate and 3/4 cup water. Cook until bubbly, stirring constantly. Pour over chicken. Cover and bake at 350°F. for 1-1/2 hours. Makes 4 servings.

CREAMY BAKED CHICKEN

1/4 cup all-purpose flour
1/2 tsp. paprika
1 tbs. salt
1/4 tsp. pepper
1/4 tsp. poultry seasoning
1 chicken, 2-1/2 to 3 lbs.,
     cut into serving pieces
1/4 cup butter
1 can (10-1/2 ozs.) cream of chicken soup
1/2 cup milk
1 tbs. chopped fresh parsley

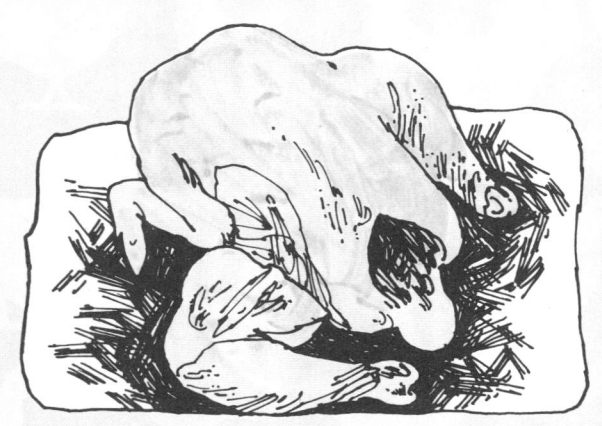

    Mix together flour, paprika, salt, pepper, and poultry seasoning in a bowl. Coat chicken pieces with mixture. Melt butter and pour into shallow baking dish. Arrange chicken in single layer in dish. Bake 30 to 40 minutes at 350°F., turning once. Combine soup and milk. Pour over chicken and sprinkle with parsley. Bake 30 to 40 minutes more. Makes 4 servings.

POPOVER CHICKEN-TARRAGON CASSEROLE

Children love the puffy, flaky "pastry" that tops this baked chicken stew.

1 tbs. vegetable oil
1 chicken, 2-1/2 to 3 lbs., cut into serving pieces
1/2 tsp. salt
1/4 tsp. pepper

3 eggs
1-1/2 cups milk
2 tbs. melted butter
1-1/2 cups all purpose flour
1 tsp. dried tarragon

Pour oil into large skillet. Place over medium-high heat. Add chicken and brown well on all sides. Sprinkle with salt and pepper. Place chicken in greased, shallow 2-quart baking dish. In mixing bowl, beat eggs. Add milk and melted butter. Mix well. Stir flour, tarragon and salt into egg mixture. Beat until smooth. Pour over chicken. Bake at 350°F. for 60 to 70 minutes. Makes 4 servings.

EASY CHICKEN POT PIE

Don't let the reputation of frozen chicken pot pies stop you from trying this great casserole. This is so much better than its frozen "cousin" you won't believe they are related.

3 tbs. butter or margarine
1/2 cup chopped onion
1/4 cup all-purpose flour
1/2 tsp. salt
1/8 tsp. freshly ground pepper
1/2 tsp. poultry seasoning

2 cups chicken broth
2 cups cooked, chopped chicken
1 cup frozen peas and carrots, cooked and drained
4 refrigerated, unbaked biscuits

Melt butter in skillet over medium heat. Saute onion in butter 8 to 10 minutes, stirring constantly. Blend in flour, salt, pepper and poultry seasoning. Gradually add broth. Stir constantly while mixture thickens. Add chicken, peas and carrots. Heat until boiling. Pour into 1-1/2-quart casserole dish. Slice biscuits into quarters. Place on top of chicken mixture. Bake at 450°F. for 8 to 10 minutes, until biscuits are browned and done. Makes 4 servings.

CHICKEN SOUP

Chicken Consomme 64
Chicken Corn Chowder 65
Chicken and Cucumber Soup 66
Chicken Giblet Soup 67
Chicken Gumbo 68
Chilled Senegalese Chicken Soup 69
Cock-a-Leekie Soup 70
Homemade Chicken Broth or Bouillon 71

CHICKEN CONSOMME

Consomme comes from the French word meaning "to boil down." It is a strong soup made by reducing broth and then clarifying to make it sparkling clear. An appropriate curtain raiser for any formal meal.

1 recipe Homemade Chicken Broth, page 71

To make consomme, reduce broth by boiling uncovered to one half its original volume. When reduced, clarify consomme in the following manner: For each quart of consomme place 2 egg whites **and** their crushed shells in large bowl. Beat until frothy and about double their original volume. Pour beaten egg whites and shells into consomme and bring back to rolling boil, stirring. Immediately remove from heat and allow to rest 5 to 10 minutes. This will allow egg whites and shells to rise to top. The impurities in the soup will be clinging to them. Next, line a wire strainer with a damp layer of muslin or cheesecloth. Place strainer over a large bowl. Gently ladle consomme into strainer. Soup will slowly drip through cloth and be clear. Re-heat and serve immediately. Note: if desired, consomme can be chilled until jellied, and served on a bed of lettuce, garnished with sprig of parsley or watercress.

CHICKEN CORN CHOWDER

This chowder originated in the Midwest, where corn fields abound. Here's a delicious modern version.

4 strips bacon	1 can (8 ozs.) whole kernel corn, drained
1 cup chopped onion	1 can (8 ozs.) cream-style corn
2 cups cubed potatoes	1 cup light cream or milk
2 cups chicken broth	1/4 tsp. pepper
2 cups diced cooked chicken	chopped fresh parsley

Fry bacon in skillet until crisp. Drain on paper towels. When cool, crumble. Drain and discard all but 2 tablespoons drippings. Saute onions in skillet over medium heat in drippings until tender, about 8 to 10 minutes. In Dutch oven combine onions, potatoes and chicken broth. Bring to boil. Reduce heat and simmer until potatoes are tender, about 15 minutes. Add chicken, whole corn, cream-style corn, light cream and pepper. Heat thoroughly. Garnish each serving with crumbled bacon bits and parsley. Makes 4 to 6 servings.

CHICKEN AND CUCUMBER SOUP

A fresh, crunchy soup that's quick to prepare. Taste a small piece of cucumber before you add them to the soup. If they are bitter, throw them away. Use only mild and sweet cucumbers in this soup.

2 whole cucumbers
1 cup chopped cooked chicken
4 cups chicken broth
3 tbs. sherry

Wash and peel cucumbers. Cut off a small piece and taste it. If bitter, discard. Use only mild, sweet cucumbers. Cut each cucumber lengthwise and remove the seeds with a spoon. Discard seeds. Cut cucumbers into thin slices. Bring chicken broth to a boil in a large saucepan. Add chopped chicken and cucumbers. Simmer for 15 minutes. Add sherry and correct seasonings. Serve hot or cold. Makes 4 to 6 servings.

CHICKEN GIBLET SOUP

1 lb. giblets (hearts and gizzards only)
4 cups chicken broth
3 tbs. butter
1 onion, chopped
1 celery stalk, chopped
1/2 green pepper, chopped
1 garlic clove, minced
2 tbs. all-purpose flour
1 tsp. prepared mustard
salt and pepper

Rinse giblets. Pour broth into large saucepan. Add giblets and simmer 1 hour. Melt butter in saucepan over medium heat. Saute onion, celery, pepper and garlic until tender, about 6 to 8 minutes. Reduce heat. Add flour. Cook 2 minutes, stirring constantly. Remove giblets from saucepan. Slice giblets and return to broth. Stir in sauteed vegetables and mustard. Add salt and pepper. Cook one minute longer, serve hot. Makes 4 servings.

CHICKEN GUMBO

Creole gumbos are dishes which use okra for flavoring and thickening. Okra is a bean or seed pod, which is the color of string beans, but about 3 to 4 inches in length. The pods have ridges which make slices of okra appear slightly octagonal in shape. Believed to have originated in West Africa, they were brought to the United States during the slave trade.

1 tbs. butter
1 onion, finely chopped
1/2 cup celery, finely chopped
4 cups chicken broth
1/2 green pepper, finely chopped

1 cup cooked or canned okra
1/2 cup chopped, cooked chicken
1 tsp. salt
1/2 tsp. pepper
1 can (16 ozs.) tomatoes

Melt butter in skillet over medium heat. Saute onion and celery in butter for 7 to 8 minutes, stirring constantly. Add chicken broth, green pepper, okra, chicken, salt, pepper, and tomatoes. Bring to boil, then reduce heat and simmer for 45 minutes. Makes 4 to 6 servings.

CHILLED SENEGALESE CHICKEN SOUP

3 tbs. butter
2 onions, chopped
2 stalks celery, chopped
2 apples, peeled, cored and chopped
1 to 1-1/4 tbs. curry powder
1/4 cup all-purpose flour

4 cups chicken broth
dash chili powder
salt
2 cups light cream or milk
3/4 cup diced, cooked chicken, chilled

Melt butter in large saucepan over medium heat. Saute onion, celery and apples 6 to 8 minutes, stirring occasionally. Add curry powder, cook, stirring for a few minutes. Do not allow curry to brown. Add flour, cook 1 minute, stirring constantly. Stir in chicken broth gradually. Cook, stirring constantly, until slightly thickened. Add chili powder and salt. Cool slightly. Pour into blender jar and puree. Chill. Before serving, stir in light cream and chilled chicken meat. Makes 6 servings.

COCK-A-LEEKIE SOUP

A rich soup of Scottish origin. The prunes add a delicate and slightly sweet flavor.

2 lbs. boneless beef shank
3 dozen leeks
1 stewing chicken, 4 to 5 lbs.
3 quarts cold water
1 tbs. salt
1 tsp. pepper
1 cup pitted prunes, cut into small pieces

    Cut beef into 5 or 6 pieces. Wash leeks very well, making sure to remove sand. Slice them thinly, including 3 inches of the darker green leaves. Put chicken, beef, leeks, water, salt and pepper into a Dutch oven. Simmer 3 hours. Check occasionally. Remove beef and chicken. Add prunes, simmer one hour longer. When meats are cool, remove bones and skin from chicken and gristle from beef. Dice meats. Return to soup. Taste for salt, soup may need quite a bit. Skim fat. Simmer 15 minutes longer. Makes 8 to 10 servings.

HOMEMADE CHICKEN BROTH OR BOUILLON

Chicken broth or bouillon is stronger than chicken stock. Stock is made using only bones and vegetables. Broth can be made by reducing stock or by starting with the entire chicken. If only broth is desired, use chicken meat for salads or other cooked chicken dishes.

1 stewing chicken, 4 to 5 lbs.
6 cups cold water
1 carrot, sliced
1 onion, sliced
2 celery stalks, with leaves
1/2 bay leaf
6 whole peppercorns
1-1/2 tsp. salt

Put all ingredients in Dutch oven. Bring to boil, cover and lower heat. Simmer 2 hours. Remove chicken. Cool broth. Skim and discard fat. Strain broth. Makes about 1 quart.

CHICKEN STEWS

Chicken Cacciatore 74
Chicken Calabrian 76
Chicken Paprika 77
Chicken Stew, Corsican Style 78
Chicken Stew with Dumplings 80
Chickpea-Lemon Chicken Stew 79
Fried Chicken Stew 82
New Brunswick Chicken Stew 83

CHICKEN CACCIATORE

This chicken, simmered in a rich, red sauce, is best served over hot spaghetti. The trick to cooking perfect spaghetti noodles or any pasta is to pour about a tablespoon of oil into the boiling, salted water with the pasta. Test frequently during cooking. All pasta should be cooked just until it offers only the slightest resistance to your teeth, when you bite it. This is called "al dente."

Complete this meal with a tossed green salad, French bread and dry red wine.

1 chicken, 2-1/2 to 3 lbs., cut into serving pieces
1 cup all-purpose flour
3 tbs. olive oil
3 tbs. butter or margarine
1 medium-sized onion, chopped
1/2 lb. small mushrooms, sliced
2 tsp. chopped fresh parsley
1 clove garlic, mashed
1 cup dry white wine
1 can (10-3/4 ozs.) spaghetti sauce with mushrooms
2 bay leaves
1/2 tsp. salt
1/2 tsp. pepper
4 ozs. dry spaghetti

Dredge chicken pieces in flour, coat well on all sides. Heat olive oil in large skillet over medium-high heat. Saute chicken until well browned on all sides. Remove chicken from skillet and set aside. Add butter to skillet. Saute onion and mushrooms until lightly browned, about 5 minutes. Add parsley, garlic and wine. Stir to scrape browned bits from bottom of skillet. Return chicken to skillet. Cover and simmer 10 minutes. Add spaghetti sauce, bay leaves, salt and pepper. Cover and simmer 35 minutes, or until chicken is tender. Remove bay leaves. Skim and discard fat. Meanwhile, cook the spaghetti in boiling, salted water until it is just tender, or "al dente." Drain spaghetti well. To serve, arrange noodles on a serving platter. Place chicken on top of noodles and spoon sauce over the chicken pieces. Makes 4 servings.

CHICKEN CALABRIAN

One of Italy's classic chicken dishes. On an attractive platter, the figs, orange slices and parsley create tremendous visual appeal.

2 chickens, 2-1/2 to 3 lbs. each, quartered
1/4 cup olive oil
1-1/2 tsp. salt
1 tsp. dried oregano
2 tsp. minced fresh parsley

2 cloves garlic, minced
1 cup dry white wine
3 tbs. lemon juice
1 can (17 ozs.) Kadota figs, drained
1 orange cut into 1/4-inch slices
1/2 cup sherry

Brush chicken with olive oil. Combine salt, oregano, parsley and garlic in a bowl. Mix well. Roll chicken in mixture. Place in shallow baking dish, skin side up. Bake, uncovered at 400°F. for 50 to 55 minutes, turning once during cooking. Combine wine and lemon juice. Use to baste chicken often during cooking. Meanwhile, prick figs with fork. Marinate figs and orange slices in sherry while chicken cooks. Five to ten minutes before chicken is done, skim and discard fat. Add figs and orange slices. Makes 4 servings.

CHICKEN PAPRIKA

3 chicken legs
3 chicken breasts
1/4 cup all-purpose flour
1/4 tsp. salt
2 tbs. oil
1/4 cup diced onions

3/4 cup hot water
2 tsp. lemon juice
3 tbs. all-purpose flour
1-1/2 cups sour cream
2 cups cooked noodles
2 tsp. paprika

Skin, bone and remove fat from chicken. Cut pieces in half. Combine 1/4 cup flour and salt in a bowl. Roll chicken in mixture. Heat oil in large skillet on medium-high heat. Add chicken and brown well on all sides. Add onions, hot water and lemon juice. Cover, and simmer 40 minutes until chicken is tender. Skim and discard fat. Blend 3 tablespoons flour with 1/2 cup of sour cream. Blend into chicken mixture. Stir in remaining sour cream and noodles. Simmer 5 minutes. Add paprika and mix well. Serve hot. Makes 6 servings.

CHICKEN STEW, CORSICAN STYLE

A simple and piquant dish. Do not add any salt until the dish is finished cooking. The bacon and olives impart a saltiness of their own.

4 tbs. olive oil
1 whole roasting chicken, about 3 lbs.
5 slices bacon, diced
1/4 lb. whole button mushrooms
1 cup pitted black olives, drained
1 lb. tomatoes, chopped
1/4 cup brandy
1 lb. new potatoes, peeled
sugar, salt and pepper

Pour 2 tablespoons of oil in Dutch oven or large skillet. Place over medium-high heat. Brown whole chicken on all sides. After chicken has sauteed for 5 minutes, add bacon and mushrooms. Cook 5 to 10 more minutes. Add olives, tomatoes and brandy. Cover and simmer for 1 hour, or until chicken is tender. Meanwhile, in frying pan, brown new potatoes lightly in remaining 2 tablespoons of olive oil. Add potatoes to Dutch oven. Cook for another 1/2 hour. Transfer to a serving dish. Skim and discard fat from sauce. Add sugar, salt and pepper to taste. Pour sauce over chicken and serve. Makes 4 servings.

CHICKEN-LEMON CHICKEN STEW

The turmeric lends this whole, stewed chicken a lovely golden-yellow color.

1 whole chicken, 3-1/2 to 4 lbs.
3 tbs. vegetable oil
1 onion, finely chopped
4 cloves garlic, minced
2 tsp. turmeric

1/2 tsp. **EACH** salt and pepper
1 to 2 quarts chicken stock
1 can (15 ozs.) chickpeas or garbanzo beans
juice of two lemons

Remove excess fat from chicken cavity. Truss chicken (see page 28). In Dutch oven heat oil to medium-high. Add onion and garlic. Saute until translucent, about 4 minutes. Add 1 teaspoon turmeric, salt and pepper. Cook one more minute. Rub chicken with remaining turmeric. Add chicken to pot and sear on all sides until golden-yellow. Add just enough stock to cover chicken. Add chickpeas and lemon juice. Bring to boil. Reduce heat and simmer until done about 1-1/2 hours. Allow chicken to rest 5 to 10 minutse before carving. Makes 4 servings.

CHICKEN STEW WITH DUMPLINGS

1 stewing chicken, 4-1/2 to 5 lbs.,
    cut into serving pieces
2 onions, sliced
5 carrots, sliced
3 to 4 celery ribs
2 whole cloves garlic, peeled

1 bay leaf
1 tsp. thyme **OR** sage
2 tsp. salt
1 tsp. pepper
chicken stock (about 4 cups)
Dumplings (next page)

    Place all ingredients in a very large pot or Dutch oven. Add enough stock to completely cover chicken. Bring to boil, partially cover and simmer for 2 to 2-1/2 hours, or until chicken is tender. Skim and discard fat from cooking liquid every 30 minutes. Start preparing dumpling batter about 30 minutes before stew is done. Using a large tablespoon, drop dough directly onto chicken in boiling stew. Cover and return to boil. Lower heat. Simmer 12 to 15 minutes without lifting cover. Remove dumplings and chicken to platter. Spoon broth over dumplings before serving. Makes 6 to 8 servings.

DUMPLINGS

Try these dumplings in beef stew too.

1 cup all-purpose flour
2 tsp. baking powder
1/2 tsp. salt
2 tbs. snipped fresh parsley
1 egg
1/3 cup milk
2 tbs. butter

Prepare dumplings about 30 minutes before chicken stew is done. Stir together flour, baking powder and salt. Add parsley. Mix egg, milk, and melted butter together. Add to flour mixture, stirring until just blended. Cook with chicken as directed in preceding recipe.

FRIED CHICKEN STEW

A hearty chicken stew which originated in Mainland China. Particularly satisfying on a cold day.

8 dry Chinese mushrooms
4 cups chicken stock
1/2 cup soy sauce
1/2 tsp. minced ginger
2 tbs. sugar
1 chicken, 1-1/2 to 3 lbs.,
    boned and cut into bite-sized pieces

1 cup all-purpose flour
vegetable oil for frying
2 bell peppers, cut into eighths
1 head Chinese or regular cabbage,
    cut into 1-inch pieces
2 scallions

Place mushrooms in small bowl. Cover with water. Let soak at room temperature for 1 hour. Drain. Slice finely. In large saucepan bring stock, soy sauce, ginger and sugar to boil. Dredge chicken in flour. Heat about 2 inches of oil in deep saucepan to medium-high (375°F.). Deep fry chicken pieces for 3 to 5 minutes. Remove and place chicken in simmering stock. Add mushrooms, bell peppers and Chinese cabbage. Serve in bowls and garnish with chopped scallions. Makes 4 servings.

NEW BRUNSWICK CHICKEN STEW

The addition of the bananas to this typically New England style dish gives it a Latin American flavor. Once cooked in the stew, their flavor more closely resembles potatoes than bananas.

1 chicken, 2-1/2 to 3 lbs., cut into serving pieces
1 tbs. salt
10 peppercorns
1 tbs. minced onion
1 bay leaf

1 can (28 ozs.) tomatoes
1 pkg. (10 ozs.) frozen corn
1 pkg. (10 ozs.) frozen lima beans
1 tsp. dried basil, crumbled
2 green-ripe bananas

Place chicken, salt, peppercorns and onion in a large kettle or Dutch oven. Cover all with 2 quarts of water. Skim and discard fat. Strain broth. Add tomatoes, corn, lima beans and basil to kettle, along with 3 cups of strained broth. Bring to boil. Remove skin and bones from chicken, dice meat. Peel and cut bananas into 1/2-inch chunks. Add chicken and bananas to soup. Cover and simmer 30 to 35 minutes. Makes 6 servings.

CHICKEN BREASTS

Basic Chicken Breast Cutlets........ 86
Sesame Chicken Cutlets 87
Chicken Breasts a la Normande 88
Chicken Breasts Picatta........... 89
Chicken Breasts in Rum Crumbs..... 90
Chicken Breasts Savoyarde......... 92
Chicken Breasts Veronique......... 91

BASIC CHICKEN BREAST CUTLETS

Here are some tips for producing perfect chicken breast cutlets. Pound them thin, being careful not to tear them. Saute the cutlets quickly, so that they stay tender and succulent. It is extremely important not to dry out the breasts by overcooking.

2 chicken breasts, skinned, boned and halved
1/4 cup all-purpose flour
salt and pepper
1 egg

1/2 cup bread crumbs
3 tbs. butter
2 tbs. cognac or brandy (optional)
parsley and lemon wedges for garnish

Place each breast half between 2 pieces of waxed paper. Flatten to thickness of 1/4-inch. Mix flour, salt and pepper together in a bowl. In another bowl, beat egg. Dip each breast in flour mixture, then egg, then crumbs. Chill at least one hour before sauteeing. Melt butter in large skillet over medium-high heat. Add breasts and saute 3 to 4 minutes, turning occasionally. If desired, warm cognac in separate pan. Pour over breasts. Carefully ignite. Gently shake pan until flames subside. Garnish with parsley and lemon wedges, if desired. Makes 4 servings.

SESAME CHICKEN CUTLETS

The toasted sesame seeds add an interesting dimension to this basic recipe.

1 egg
1 tsp. salt
1/4 tsp. pepper
1 tbs. lemon juice
1 tbs. grated fresh lemon peel
2 tbs. toasted sesame seeds
1/2 cup fine dry bread crumbs

2 chicken breasts, skinned, boned, and halved
1/4 cup all-purpose flour
1/4 cup butter or oil for frying
lemon slices
chopped parsley

Beat egg in bowl. Add salt, pepper, lemon juice and lemon peel. Set aside. Mix sesame seeds and bread crumbs together. Place each breast half between 2 pieces of waxed paper and flatten to thickness of 1/4-inch with mallet. Dip breasts in flour, then egg mixture, then crumbs. Place in single layer on waxed paper. Refrigerate at least 1/2 hour before cooking. Melt butter in large skillet over medium-high heat. Add breasts and cook until golden brown on both sides, 3 to 4 minutes. Serve on warm platter. Garnish with lemon slices and parsley. Makes 4 servings.

CHICKEN BREASTS A LA NORMANDE

A variation of the Chicken with Cream and Calvados Recipe.

2 chicken breasts, skinned, boned and halved
flour
1/4 cup oil
3/4 cup brandy (preferably apple brandy)
1/2 cup whipping cream
2 tsp. butter or margarine
2 small green apples
2 to 4 tbs. sugar

Roll breasts in flour. Heat oil in skillet to medium-high. Add breasts and saute 1 to 2 minutes per side, or until golden. Remove breasts and discard oil. Add 1/2 cup brandy to skillet and return breasts. Place over high heat, **ignite carefully,** then immediately cover to put out flame. Again, remove breasts. Add cream to skillet and reduce liquid, by boiling, to half its original volume. Add butter and shake pan until butter melts. Peel, core and slice apples thinly. Stir sugar and remaining brandy into skillet. Add apple slices. Bring to boil and cook one minute. Place breasts on warm serving plate, surround with apples and top with sauce. Makes 4 servings.

CHICKEN BREASTS PICATTA

The Madeira, lemon juice and capers form a piquant counterpoint to the breasts.

2 chicken breasts, skinned, boned and halved
1/4 cup all-purpose flour
3/4 tsp. salt
1/4 tsp. paprika
3 tbs. olive oil

2 tbs. butter
2 tbs. Madeira wine
2 tbs. lemon juice
1/2 lemon, thinly sliced
2 tbs. capers
2 tbs. chopped fresh parsley

Place each breast half between 2 pieces of waxed paper and flatten to thickness of 1/4-inch with mallet. Mix together flour, salt and paprika in plastic bag. Shake each breast in bag. Heat oil and butter in large skillet over medium-high heat. Saute breasts one minute on each side, or until golden. Remove to warm platter. Drain and discard all but two tablespoons butter mixture. Add Madeira to skillet. Cook over medium heat, stirring to dissolve bits which have adhered to skillet bottom. Add lemon juice. Heat briefly. Return breasts and lemon slices to re-heat. Add capers and parsley, serve. Makes 4 servings.

CHICKEN BREASTS IN RUM CRUMBS

A warm, buttery delight! The crusty covering of "rum crumbs" surrounds the chicken breasts. These envelope a chestnut and chutney filling

2 chicken breasts, skinned, boned and halved
1/4 cup **PLUS** 1 tbs. rum
1/2 cup breadcrumbs
1/4 cup butter
2 tbs. chutney, with liquid
2 tbs. pureed marrons (chestnut spread)

Place each breast half between 2 pieces of waxed paper and flatten to thickness of 1/4-inch with mallet. Pour 1/4 cup rum into small bowl. Dip each chicken breast half into rum, then into crumbs. Melt butter in skillet over medium-high heat. Saute each chicken one minute per side, until golden. Meanwhile, mix chutney and marron with 1 tablespoon rum. Warm in small saucepan. Spread mixture onto half of chicken pieces. Top with other sauteed chicken pieces. Serve hot. Makes 4 servings.

CHICKEN BREASTS VERONIQUE

Another French classic. This combination of chicken, cream and grapes is a true inspiration.

4 chicken breasts, skinned, boned and halved
salt
2 tbs. **EACH** butter and orange marmalade

1/2 tsp. tarragon
1/2 cup dry white wine
2 tsp. cornstarch
1/2 cup whipping cream
1-1/2 cups seedless grapes

Lightly salt breasts. Melt butter in large skillet over medium heat. Add breasts and saute 1 to 2 minutes on each side, or until golden. Add marmalade, tarragon and wine to skillet. Blend, cover and simmer 15 minutes. Transfer chicken to warm platter. Blend cornstarch with 4 tablespoons water. Add whipping cream to skillet and quickly bring to rolling boil. Stir in cornstarch paste. Add grapes. Bring to boil again. Pour sauce over breasts and serve. Makes 6 to 8 servings.

CHICKEN BREASTS SAVOYARDE

A truly sumptuous recipe. My wife's favorite.

Sauce (see next page)
2 tbs. vegetable oil
1 tbs. butter or margarine
1 medium onion, sliced
1 tsp. dried tarragon
1/2 tsp. thyme

4 chicken breasts, skinned boned and halved
1/2 cup dry white wine
1 tsp. salt
1/4 tsp. pepper
1 can (8 ozs.) artichoke bottoms
1/4 cup chopped parsley

Prepare sauce and set aside. In large skillet, heat oil and butter over medium-low heat. Add onion, tarragon and thyme. Cook until onions are tender, about 8 to 10 minutes, stirring frequently. Add breasts, about half at a time. Do not crowd them or they won't brown properly. Saute 6 to 8 minutes, turning once. Add wine, salt and pepper. Cover and simmer 5 minutes more. Heat artichoke bottoms gently in their own liquid, drain. Arrange chicken breasts in shallow lightly greased baking dish. Place artichokes around chicken. Pour sauce over chicken. Place under broiler to heat through and brown, about 5 minutes. Sprinkle with parsley. Makes 8 servings.

SAUCE

1 tbs. butter or margarine
1 tbs. all-purpose flour
3/4 cup dry white wine
1/2 cup chicken broth
1/2 cup sour cream
1/2 cup grated Parmesan cheese
1/2 tbs. prepared mustard
1/4 tsp. pepper

In saucepan, melt butter over medium heat. Stir in flour. Cook, while stirring constantly, until mixture bubbles for 30 seconds. Gradually stir in white wine, chicken broth and sour cream. Simmer 5 minutes, or just until boiling. Add cheese, mustard and pepper. Simmer 5 minutes more, stirring. Remove from heat. Use as directed in recipe above.

CHICKEN WITH WINES AND SPIRITS

Baked Orange-Rum Chicken 96
Chicken Cooked in
    Burgundy Wine (Coq Au Vin) 98
Chicken with Cream and Calvados . . . 99
Chicken with Cream, Wine
    and Mushrooms 100
Chicken-Ham Marsala 102
Chicken in Sake Sauce 103
Chicken Simmered in Beer 104
Spirited Chicken in Clay 105

BAKED ORANGE-RUM CHICKEN

A great dish to serve on a warm summer's evening. The combination of rum and orange flavoring are reminiscent of Caribbean cuisine.

1/4 cup rum
2 tbs. butter
2 tbs. firmly packed brown sugar
2 tbs. frozen orange juice concentrate
3/4 tsp. salt
1/8 tsp. pepper
1/4 tsp. ground ginger
1 chicken, 2-1/2 to 3 lbs., cut into serving pieces

In small saucepan combine rum, butter, brown sugar, orange juice concentrate, salt, pepper and ginger. Place over medium heat, until sugar dissolves. Brush pieces of chicken with mixture. Arrange chicken, skin side up, in a large shallow baking dish. Bake, uncovered at 375°F. for 50 to 60 minutes, basting once with rum mixture during baking process and once again just before serving. Makes 4 serving.

CHICKEN AMARETTO

Lovers of the almond-flavored liqueur "Amaretto" will especially like this simple recipe. They won't have to wait until after dinner to savor its goodness.

6 chicken breast halves,
   boned and skinned
1 tsp. salt
1/2 tsp. pepper
1/4 tsp. **EACH** garlic powder and curry powder
1/4 cup flour and butter

1/2 lb. fresh mushrooms, sliced
1/4 cup Amaretto liqueur
grated rind and juice of 1 lemon
1 tbs. cornstarch
1-1/2 cups chicken broth

Cut chicken into 1-inch wide strips. Mix salt, pepper, garlic powder, curry powder and flour together in plastic bag. Shake chicken pieces in bag with mixture. Melt butter in a large skillet over medium-high heat. Add chicken pieces and saute quickly. Reduce heat to medium-low. Add mushrooms, Amaretto, lemon rind, and juice. Simmer 5 minutes. Mix cornstarch and 2 tablespoons water to form paste. Blend paste with chicken broth. Stir mixture into skillet with chicken. Cook over low heat, stirring constantly until mixture bubbles and thickens. Makes 6 to 8 servings.

CHICKEN COOKED IN BURGUNDY WINE (COQ AU VIN)

1/2 cup butter
3 slices bacon finely chopped
1 medium onion, finely sliced
1 chicken, 2-1/2 to 3 lbs., cut into serving pieces
1 tbs. flour
2 tbs. brandy
2 cups dry red wine
1 bay leaf
1/4 tsp. dried thyme
1 tbs. chopped fresh parsley
1 tbs. salt
1/2 tsp. pepper
1/8 tsp. ground nutmeg
1 cup chopped mushrooms, sauteed in butter

Melt 1/4 cup butter in a Dutch oven over medium heat. Saute bacon and onion until transparent, about 5 minutes. Remove bacon and onion with slotted spoon and reserve. Add chicken and brown on all sides in remaining fat. Sprinkle with flour. Add brandy, wine, bay leaf, thyme, parsley, salt, pepper and nutmeg. Cover and bake at 350°F. for 40 minutes. Skim and discard fat. Stir in reserved onion, bacon and mushrooms. Cover and return to oven. Bake 5 to 10 minutes more. Stir remaining butter into sauce. Serve with noodles or mashed potatoes. Makes 4 servings.

CHICKEN WITH CREAM AND CALVADOS

Every hotel in Normandy, France has a different method of preparing this famous dish. Here is my favorite rendition.

3/4 cup butter
2 chickens, 2-1/2 to 3 lbs. each, quartered
1/4 cup warmed Calvados (apple brandy)
2 small white onions, minced
1 tbs. chopped fresh parsley
salt and pepper
1/3 cup plus 1 tbs. **EACH** apple cider and cream

In large skillet melt butter over medium heat. Add chicken, and saute for 20 minutes. Add Calvados and carefully ignite. When flame has subsided, add onions, parsley, salt, pepper and cider. Cover and cook over low heat until chicken is tender, about 20 minutes. Place chicken on platter in warm (200°F.) oven. Skim and discard fat from sauce. Slowly stir cream into skillet. Heat thoroughly. Serve sauce over chicken. Makes 4 servings.

CHICKEN WITH CREAM, WINE AND MUSHROOMS

A great dish to serve company. Since it already contains vegetables, finish the meal with a salad and rolls.

2 chickens, 2-1/2 to 3 lbs. each, cut into serving pieces
2 carrots, sliced
2 onions, chopped
2 cups chicken broth
1/4 cup chopped parsley
1/2 tsp. thyme
1 bay leaf
2 whole cloves
4 peppercorns
1/4 cup butter
Cream Sauce (see next page)

Bring 2 quarts of water to a boil in a Dutch oven, or large saucepan. Add chicken pieces, carrots, onion, chicken broth, parsley, thyme, bay leaf, cloves and peppercorns. Reduce heat to low and simmer until chicken is tender, about 1 hour. When chicken is done, remove it from broth and set aside to drain. Strain broth and reserve. Discard vegetables and herbs. Dry chicken pieces with paper towels. Melt butter in large skillet over medium-high heat. Saute chicken pieces on all sides. Place chicken on platter in warm (200°F.) oven. Prepare sauce.

CREAM SAUCE

1/3 cup **PLUS** 1 tbs. butter
1/4 cup all-purpose flour
2 cups reserved chicken broth
1 cup dry white wine
2 egg yolks

1/4 cup cream
1/4 cup butter
1 lb. fresh mushrooms, sliced
juice of 2 lemons

Melt 1/3 cup plus 1 tablespoon butter in saucepan over medium heat. Stir in flour. Cook, stirring contantly, for 3 minutes. Gradually add chicken broth and wine. Bring mixture to a boil, while stirring. Skim and discard fat. Simmer sauce, uncovered, over low heat until its volume is reduced by half. Lightly beat together egg yolks and cream. Stir into sauce and continue cooking and stirring until sauce becomes slightly thickened, remove from heat and set aside. Melt remaining 1/4 cup butter in a large skillet. Add sliced mushrooms and saute until tender, about 5 minutes. Remove chicken pieces from oven. Spoon sauce over chicken. Surround chicken with sauteed mushrooms. Pour lemon juice over all. Makes 6 to 8 servings.

CHICKEN-HAM MARSALA

Marsala wine compliments this creamy combination of chicken and ham.

1/4 lb. cooked ham, finely chopped
6 large chicken thighs, bones removed
2 tbs. butter, melted
1/2 cup sliced mushrooms
1 can (10 ozs.) cream of mushroom soup

1 cup (1/2 pint) sour cream
1/2 cup Marsala wine
2 tsp. paprika
1 tbs. cornstarch mixed with 2 tbs. water

Divide chopped ham into 6 portions. Fill inside of chicken thighs with ham. Fold over to close, and tie, skin side out, with string (or secure with skewers). Pour butter into a 9-inch square baking dish. Roll chicken in butter and place in dish. Combine mushrooms, soup, sour cream and Marsala in saucepan. Place over medium-high heat, stirring constantly. As soon as mixture begins to bubble, remove it from heat. Pour mixture over chicken. Sprinkle with paprika. Bake uncovered at 450°F. for 15 minutes. Cover and reduce heat to 350°F. Bake 30 minutes more. Remove chicken to serving platter. Pour sauce into saucepan. Simmer until warm. Add cornstarch paste. Stir until thickened. Pour over chicken and serve. Makes 4 to 6 servings.

CHICKEN IN SAKE SAUCE

A mild and subtle dish which is simple to prepare.

1 cup flour
5 **EACH** chicken legs, and thighs
1/4 cup vegetable oil
2 cans (10 ozs. each) cream of mushroom soup
1/2 cup milk
5 ounces Sake (rice wine)

Roll chicken pieces in flour. Heat vegetable oil in large skillet over medium-high heat. Add chicken pieces and saute until brown on all sides. Mix soup, milk and Sake together. Arrange chicken pieces in shallow baking dish. Pour sauce over chicken and bake, uncovered, at 350°F. for 40 to 50 minutes. Makes 4 to 5 servings.

CHICKEN SIMMERED IN BEER

1/4 cup butter
1 chicken, 2-1/2 to 3 lbs., cut into serving pieces
salt and pepper
6 green onions, finely chopped
1 large carrot, grated
1 bay leaf
1/4 tsp. dried thyme
1 bottle (12 ozs.) beer
1 cup stewed tomatoes, drained
1 tbs. flour

Melt butter in skillet over medium-high heat. Add chicken, sprinkle with salt and pepper, and saute on all sides. Add green onions, carrot, bay leaf and thyme. Sprinkle with 1/2 teaspoon salt. Pour in beer. Cover and reduce heat. Simmer until chicken is tender, about 1-1/2 hours. Remove to warm platter. Skim and discard fat. Add tomatoes. Mix flour with 4 tablespoons water until lumps disappear and add to sauce. Cook until thickened. Serve chicken covered with sauce. Makes 4 servings.

SPIRITED CHICKEN IN CLAY

This recipe was especially designed for the popular clay roasting dishes. Chicken is flavorful, moist and delicious prepared this way.

1 tsp. salt
1 roasting chicken, 4 to 5 lbs.
1/4 cup butter
1 tbs. **PLUS** 1 tsp. grated orange rind
3 tbs. lime juice

1 tsp. Worcestershire sauce
2 tbs. orange liqueur
1/3 cup **PLUS** 1 tbs. orange marmalade
2 tbs. brandy

Salt cavity of chicken. Melt butter in large skillet over medium-high heat. Add chicken and saute on all sides. Remove chicken from heat. Combine orange rind, lime juice, Worcestershire sauce, orange liqueur, marmalade and brandy. Pour over chicken and let stand one hour. Soak clay crockery dish in water for 10 minutes. Line dish with foil because sugar in recipe will encrust bottom. Place chicken in dish. Cover tightly and roast chicken at 400°F. for one hour. Spoon sauce over chicken and roast 30 minutes more. Makes 4 to 6 servings.

CHICKEN FLAVORED WITH SPICES

Chicken Curry. 108
Chicken with Vinegar Sauce 110
Garlic Chicken 112
Ginger and Anise Chicken. 111
Mustard Chicken Surprise. 114
Sour Cream Baked Chicken 115

CHICKEN CURRY

Ceylon is the birthplace of this spicy curry. The proper way to serve this dish is to pass the rice first. Spread it generously on your plate. Next, place a few pieces of chicken and some sauce over the rice. Then pass a variety of condiments to top the dish. Some traditional ones are: raisins, peanuts, chopped hard cooked egg, flaked coconut, chutney, pickles and sliced banana.

1 tsp. ground coriander **OR** curry powder
1/2 tsp. chili powder
1/4 tsp. ground saffron
pinch of ginger
1 tsp. salt
1 chicken, 2-1/2 to 3 lbs., cut into serving pieces
3 tbs. vegetable oil

2 tbs. minced onion
1 cup milk
1/2 cup flaked coconut
1 bay leaf
1/2-inch piece of cinnamon stick
1/2 tsp. **EACH** cloves, cardamon and cinnamon
rice to serve 4
assorted condiments

Mix coriander, chili powder, saffron, ginger and salt together well in a large bowl.

Roll chicken, one piece at a time in spice mixture. Pour oil in large skillet and place over medium-high heat. Saute chicken pieces in skillet, being careful not to crowd pieces. Cook 5 minutes. Add onions. Cook 5 minutes longer. Reduce heat to low. Add milk, coconut, bay leaf and cinnamon stick. Simmer gently for 1 hour, or until chicken is tender and sauce is thick. Remove from heat. Skim and discard fat. Sprinkle with cloves, cardamon and cinnamon. Serve with rice and pass the condiments, as described above. Makes 4 servings.

CHICKEN WITH VINEGAR SAUCE

A very good, fresh tasting sauce that is mildly piquant.

1 chicken, 3 to 4 lbs., cut into serving pieces
1 cup all-purpose flour
1/2 tsp. pepper
1/2 cup butter

4 cloves garlic, chopped
1 tbs. tomato paste
1/2 cup tarragon-flavored vinegar
veal or beef stock
1 tbs. Dijon mustard

Roll chicken pieces in flour which has been mixed with salt and pepper. In deep skillet melt half of butter over medium-high heat. Saute chicken in butter until lightly browned. Add onion, garlic, tomato paste, vinegar and wine. Add enough stock to barely cover chicken. Bring to boil. Reduce heat, cover and simmer 30 minutes. Next, transfer chicken to warm serving dish. Skim and discard fat. Correct seasonings and return liquid to boil. Remove from heat. Stir in remaining butter and mustard. Pour sauce over chicken and serve. Makes 4 servings.

GINGER AND ANISE CHICKEN

3/4 cup soy sauce
1 tbs. honey
1/2 cup firmly packed brown sugar
1-1/2 cups water
2 tbs. minced fresh ginger
3 cloves garlic, minced

1 star anise (if available)
1/4 cup chopped green onions
2 tbs. sherry
1 chicken 2-1/2 to 3 lbs., whole
2 tbs. cornstarch mixed with 4 tbs. water

Combine soy sauce, honey, brown sugar, water, ginger, garlic, star anise, green onions and sherry in large cooking pot. Bring to boil. Simmer, stirring for 2 minutes. Add chicken, including liver and gizzard. Cover and simmer 40 minutes, or until chicken is tender. Remove chicken from pot and let stand at room temperature for 30 minutes to cool. Remove flesh from bones. Discard bones. Cut into bite-sized pieces with cleaver or sharp knife. Arrange on platter. Add cornstarch paste to sauce. Bring to boil. Simmer until mixture thickens. Pour over chicken. Makes 4 servings.

GARLIC CHICKEN

Although an entire head of garlic is used in this recipe, it does not overpower the dish. Simmering the garlic, as you would a vegetable, lessens its pungent flavor. Mash the cloves and stir them into the sauce; or use the whole cloves to garnish the chicken.

1 chicken, 3 lbs., cut into serving pieces
salt and pepper
3 tbs. butter
1 whole head of garlic (12 to 15 cloves)
1/2 tsp. dried rosemary
1/3 cup dry white wine
1/2 cup chicken stock
chopped fresh parsley for garnish

Sprinkle chicken with salt and pepper. Melt butter in large ovenproof skillet over medium-high heat. Saute chicken pieces until lightly browned. Cover skillet and place in a 375°F. oven for 8 minutes. Meanwhile, peel all garlic cloves, leaving them whole.

Place whole cloves in small saucepan. Add enough water to just cover garlic. Simmer for 25 minutes. Drain, being careful not to mash cloves. Add garlic, rosemary and wine to chicken. Return to oven and bake an additional 25 minutes. Remove skillet from oven. Arrange chicken and garlic on heated platter. Keep warm in 200°F. oven. Skim and discard all except 4 tablespoons of fat from skillet. Add chicken stock to skillet. Boil uncovered until reduced to one-half its origianl volume. Stir to dissolve the brown bits clinging to bottom of pan. Add garlic cloves, simmer gently for 2 minutes. Pour over chicken. Garnish with chopped parsley. Serve immediately. Makes 4 servings.

MUSTARD SURPRISE CHICKEN

The surprise in this recipe is that the two cups of mustard create an easy-to-make dish which has a mild and delicate taste.

1 frying chicken, 2-1/2 to 3 lbs., cut into serving pieces
2 cups inexpensive prepared mustard (not Dijon)
salt and pepper

Dredge chicken in mustard, coating each piece thoroughly. Sprinkle with salt and pepper. Bake in shallow, uncovered, greased baking dish for one hour at 350°F. Mustard will have formed a puff pastry-like shell around each piece of chicken. Makes 4 servings.

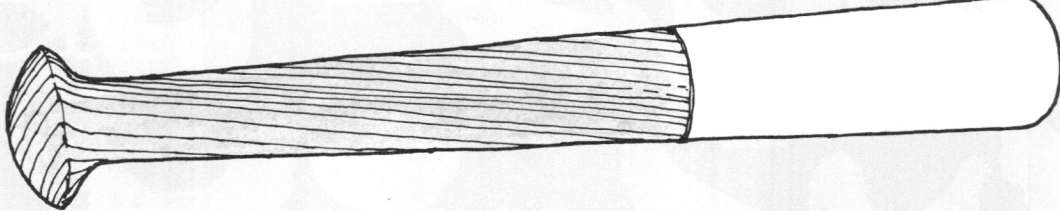

SOUR CREAM BAKED CHICKEN

A simple dish whose rich sour cream and mustard sauce qualifies it as a company meal. Prepare it with a gourmet mustard for a special treat.

1/2 cup sour cream
1/4 cup prepared mustard
1 tsp. salt
1/4 tsp. rosemary leaves, crushed
1/8 tsp. black pepper
2 chickens, 3 lbs. each, cut into serving pieces
2-1/2 cups fresh bread crumbs
1/2 cup melted butter

Combine sour cream, mustard, salt, rosemary and pepper. Mix well. Spread mixture over chicken pieces, coating well. Roll chicken in bread crumbs. Arrange in shallow baking dish. Drizzle with half of butter. Bake at 375°F. for 30 minutes. Remove from oven and drizzle with remaining butter. Bake 30 minutes more, or until chicken is golden brown and done. Makes 6 to 8 servings.

INTERNATIONAL CLASSICS

Chicken Kiev. 118
Chicken Mole 120
Deep Fried Chicken 124
Maryland Fried Chicken 125
Paella Valenciana 122
Tandoori Chicken. 119

CHICKEN KIEV

12 tbs. butter (3/4 cup)
3 eggs
2 tbs. water

6 whole chicken breasts, skinned, boned and halved (see page 12)
about 2 cups finely crumbled dry bread crumbs
vegetable oil for frying

Slice butter into 12 pieces, each about 2-inches x 1/4-inch. Chill until hard. Beat eggs and water together in bowl. Place each breast between two sheets of waxed paper. Pound with a mallet until 1/4-inch thick. Trim and discard any ragged edges. Roll each pounded breast around 1 slice of butter. Fold the right and left sides over and secure with toothpicks. Do this carefully. It's important that the butter not leak during the cooking process. Roll bundle in bread crumbs. Dip in beaten egg mixture. Roll in crumbs again. Refrigerate for at least 1 hour. Heat about 2 inches of oil in a deep skillet to medium-high, or 350°F. Carefully slip 3 or 4 bundles into the hot oil at a time. Don't try and fry them all at once. It's important not to crowd them, because the temperature of the oil will drop causing the chicken to cook too slowly and become greasy. Fry the bundles from 6 to 8 minutes, or until dark brown. Drain on paper towels. Keep warm in 200°F. oven while others fry. Makes 6 servings.

TANDOORI CHICKEN

1 chicken, 3 lbs., whole
1/2 tsp. **EACH,** salt and pepper
3/4 tsp. cayenne pepper
1-1/2 tsp. lemon juice
2 tbs. melted butter

MARINADE
3 tbs. chopped, fresh ginger
4 cloves garlic
1 tbs. whole cumin seeds
2 tbs. lemon juice
1/4 cup plain yogurt
1/2 tsp. cayenne pepper
3/4 tsp. red food coloring

    Remove skin from chicken. Slash meat on breasts and thighs with sharp knife. Mix together salt, pepper, cayenne pepper and lemon juice in a small bowl. Rub mixture over chicken and into slashes. Prepare marinade by combining all marinade ingredients in blender jar. Puree to form smooth paste. Coat chicken with marinade. Cover and refrigerate 24 hours. When ready to cook, preheat oven to 400°F. Roast chicken on rack in roasting pan or on spit for 45 minutes. Baste occasionally with melted butter and any juices remaining in marinade bowl. Increase heat to 425°F. and roast 10 to 15 minutes more without basting. Makes 4 servings.

CHICKEN MOLE

Justifiably, one of Mexico's most famous dishes. The bitter chocolate, toasted seeds and spices blend together to make a very rich, thick sauce for the chicken.

4 tbs. vegetable oil
2 chickens, 3 lbs. each,
　　cut into serving pieces
1/4 cup sesame seeds
1 cup sliced almonds
1/3 cup pumpkin seeds
2 heat and serve (crispy) taco shells
1 cup onions, chopped
2 cloves garlic

1 can (16 ozs.) tomatoes
2 cups chicken broth
1 tsp. cinnamon
1 oz. grated bitter (baking) chocolate
2 tsp. finely minced chili pepper
salt and pepper
1 tbs. sugar
2 tbs. lime juice

Pour 2 tablespoons oil in large skillet. Heat to medium-high. Add chicken pieces and brown on all sides. Remove chicken to large shallow baking dish. Cook sesame seeds, almonds and pumpkin seeds in skillet over medium heat until brown, stirring

constantly. Place nuts and seeds in blender jar and puree. Add taco shells to jar. Puree again. Add remaining 2 tablespoons of oil to skillet. Saute onions and garlic until well browned. Add to blender jar. Finally, add tomatoes, broth, cinnamon, chocolate, chili, salt, pepper, sugar and lime juice to blender jar. Puree again. Pour sauce over chicken. Cover and bake 1 hour at 375°F. Skim and discard fat. Serve with sauce spooned over chicken. Makes 8 servings.

PAELLA VALENCIANA

Worth travelling to Spain to eat. But you can cook it at home and feel as if you are in Valencia. A great party dish!

1/3 cup olive oil
1 chicken, 2-1/2 to 3 lbs.,
    cut into serving pieces
1/2 lb. pork, diced
1 tsp. salt
1/2 tsp. pepper
1 onion, chopped
1/4 tsp. saffron
2 cloves garlic, minced
1 green pepper,
    seeded and chopped

3 medium tomatoes, chopped
1-1/2 cups uncooked rice
3 cups chicken stock
1/2 lb. fresh or
    1 pkg. frozen green peas
3 pimientos, sliced
1/2 lb. firm-flesh fish fillets, cubed
3/4 lb. raw shrimp,
    shelled and deveined
10 to 12 clams, well scrubbed

In large Dutch oven heat olive oil to medium-high. Add chicken and pork. Saute until well browned. Remove with slotted spoon. Add salt, pepper, onion, saffron, garlic and green peppers. Saute until browned. Add tomatoes, rice and chicken stock. Cover and simmer 5 minutes. Return chicken and pork to Dutch oven. Cover and cook 30 minutes. Add peas, pimientos, fish and shrimp. Cover and cook 10 minutes. Meanwhile, prepare clams in separate saucepan. Place clams in saucepan with 1/2-cup water. Cover and cook over medium heat 6 to 8 minutes. Reduce heat and discard any clams that have not opened. Arrange clams in the stew. Makes 8 servings.

DEEP FRIED CHICKEN

Everyones' favorite. Although there are scores of variations, this is one of the best.

1 cup all-purpose flour
2 tsp. salt
1 tsp. black pepper

1 chicken, 2-1/2 tp 3 lbs., cut into serving pieces
lard or vegetable oil for frying (about 3 to 4 cups)

Mix flour, salt and pepper in large bowl. An hour before cooking, do not wipe chicken dry, but directly coat each piece of chicken by rolling in flour. Place pieces on wire rack and allow to stand at room temperature for 1 hour. Place a cookie sheet covered with absorbent paper towels in oven. Heat oil to 350°F. (use a frying thermometer) in deep saucepan equipped with frying basket. There should be enough fat to completely cover chicken pieces immersed in it. Carefully drop dark meat pieces into hot fat. Fry 10 to 12 minutes, turning occasionally with tongs. When done, place pieces in oven on cookie sheet to keep warm while frying remaining chicken. Fry white meat pieces for 8 to 9 minutes each, turning occasionally. Serve on warm platter. Makes 4 servings.

MARYLAND FRIED CHICKEN

One of the variations of the Deep Fried Chicken recipe given on the preceding page. Whip up some fluffy mashed potatoes to make this meal complete.

1 cup all-purpose flour
2 tsp. salt
1 tsp. black pepper
1 chicken, 2-1/2 to 3 lbs., cut into serving pieces

lard or oil for frying (about 3 to 4 cups)
3/4 cup milk
3 tbs. all-purpose flour
1 tsp. salt
3/4 cup milk

Prepare chicken according to the method for Deep Fried Chicken on the previous page. When all chicken pieces are fried, place on cookie sheet in 200°F. oven. Pour off all but 4 tablespoons lard and the brown, crumbly pieces which have fallen into lard. In bowl, mix together 3/4 cup milk, 3 tablespoons flour, and 1 teaspoon salt. Stir until well blended. Mix in additional 3/4 cup milk. Add mixture to pan containing reserved 4 tablespoons lard. Cook, stirring and scraping constantly until thickened and bubbly. Cook 2 to 3 minutes more. Pour some gravy over warm chicken and serve rest in gravy bowl. Makes 4 servings.

ORIENTAL DELICACIES

Basic Stir-Fried Chicken 128
Chicken Sauteed with
    Hoisin Sauce and Green Peppers 129
Chicken Velvet and Peas 130
Chinese Lemon Chicken 132
Paper Wrapped Chicken 134
Royal Peacock
    Silver Wrapped Chicken 135
Simmered Japanese Chicken Breasts 131

BASIC STIR-FRIED CHICKEN

1 chicken breast, boned and skinned
2 slices fresh ginger root, peeled
1 scallion
1 tbs. cornstarch
1 tbs. **EACH** sherry and water
1 lb. vegetables (celery, mushrooms, water chestnuts, peas, onions, bamboo shoots; in any combination desired)

3 tbs. vegetable oil
1 tbs. soy sauce
1/2 tsp. sugar
1 tsp. salt
1/2 cup chicken stock

Slice chicken into thin pieces. Mince ginger root and scallion. Combine with cornstarch, sherry and water. Add to chicken. Toss to coat and let stand 15 minutes. Meanwhile, slice desired vegetables. Pour 1-1/2 tablespoons oil in skillet or wok. Heat to high. Stir-fry chicken 2 to 3 minutes and remove from skillet. Heat remaining 1-1/2 tablespoons oil. Add vegetables and stir fry 1 to 2 minutes. Sprinkle with soy sauce, sugar and salt. Stir in stock. Simmer until vegetables are crisp-tender. Return chicken to re-heat. Serve at once. Makes 4 servings.

CHICKEN SAUTEED WITH HOISIN SAUCE AND GREEN PEPPERS (SZECHUAN)

This exciting dish will make you think you are eating in your favorite Szechuan Chinese restaurant.

1 tsp. salt
2 tsp. cornstarch
2 tsp. sherry
3/4 lb. raw boned chicken, diced
1/4 cup vegetable oil

1 tbs. Hoisin sauce (or substitute 2 tbs. catsup)
2 dried mushrooms, soaked and diced
1 green pepper, diced
1/2 tsp. red chili pepper, minced
1/2 cup bamboo shoots, diced

Mix salt, cornstarch and sherry. Add chicken and stir to coat well. Heat oil in skillet or wok until quite hot. Saute chicken over high heat 2 minutes. Remove chicken. Add Hoisin sauce to skillet. Cook one minute more. Add mushrooms, green pepper, chili pepper and bamboo shoots. Saute one minute. Return chicken to skillet to reheat. Serve immediately. Makes 4 servings.

CHICKEN VELVET AND PEAS

A smooth variation of basic stir-fried chicken. Serve it over rice. A fruit salad will round out the meal nicely.

2 chicken breasts, boned and skinned
2 tbs. chopped fresh ginger
3 scallions, chopped
1 tsp. sherry
2 tsp. soy sauce
6 egg whites
2 tbs. cornstarch
1/3 cup vegetable oil
6 ozs. peas or snow peas
1/4 cup chicken stock
2 ozs. cooked ham, minced

Mince chicken breasts finely. Mix ginger, scallions, sherry, soy sauce, egg whites and cornstarch until mixture is smooth. Heat oil in skillet or wok until quite hot. Add peas and stir fry 2 minutes (one minute for snow peas). Add chicken stock. Continue to cook, stirring 1-1/2 minutes. Add chicken-egg mixture. Stir fry over high heat about 2 minutes, breaking up any lumps. Serve mixture on heated platter, garnished with minced ham. Makes 4 servings.

SIMMERED JAPANESE CHICKEN BREASTS

This is a teriyaki-type of dish that doesn't require a broiler or grill. Make a big batch, the leftovers are great served cold over hot, steaming rice. This is a good dish for a crowd too.

2 chicken breasts, skinned, boned and halved
1/3 cup vegetable oil
1/3 cup soy sauce
1/4 cup sugar
1 tsp. minced fresh ginger

Bring two cups water to boiling over medium-high heat in large saucepan. Plunge breasts into boiling water for 30 seconds. Drain. Heat oil in skillet until quite hot and brown the breasts for 2 to 3 minutes. (If you are doubling or tripling the recipe, brown only 2 chicken breasts at a time). Remove breasts and pour off oil. Add soy sauce, sugar and ginger to skillet. Cook covered 5 to 6 minutes. Remove cover and simmer until sauce is syrupy. Slice breasts and serve hot or cold. Makes 4 servings.

CHINESE LEMON CHICKEN

Takes a bit of time to prepare, but the results are well worth the effort. These delicious morsels of chicken taste similar to scallops when prepared this way. Great served as an appetizer. Simply place the cubes in an attractive bowl next to a dish of toothpicks.

1 lb. chicken, boned, skinned and diced
1/2 tsp. salt
1/2 tsp. M.S.G.
2 tbs. egg custard mix (powder)
1/4 tsp. pepper
1/2 tsp. soy sauce

1 tbs. white wine
2 tsp. water
Lemon Sauce (see next page)
1/3 cup cornstarch
1 egg beaten
1/4 cup peanut oil
lemon slices for garnish

Marinate chicken for 30 minutes in mixture of salt, M.S.G., egg custard mix, pepper, soy sauce, wine and water. Meanwhile, prepare Lemon Sauce. Just before cooking chicken, add cornstarch and egg to chicken mixture. Heat oil until it is quite hot in wok or skillet. Add chicken mixture and stir fry 2 to 3 minutes until golden brown. Arrange on serving platter. Bring Lemon Sauce to boil, pour over chicken. Garnish with lemon slices. Makes 4 servings.

LEMON SAUCE

1/2 tsp. cornstarch	3 tbs. water
2 tsp. egg custard mix (powder)	1/2 tsp. salt
3 tsp. sugar	1/4 tsp. sesame oil
1/4 cup lemon juice	3 lemon slices, halved
1/2 tsp. white vinegar	

Combine cornstarch, custard mix and sugar in small suacepan. Add lemon juice, vinegar, water, salt and sesame oil. Add lemon slices. Bring to boil. Pour over cooked chicken.

PAPER WRAPPED CHICKEN

Wrapped chicken recipes are usually served as appetizers. The following two recipes are good examples of Chinese hors d'oeuvres cuisine.

4 dried Chinese mushrooms
1/2 lb. raw chicken, boned and diced
2 tbs. soy sauce
1 tbs. dry sherry
1 tbs. sugar

sixteen 6-inch squares of waxed paper
2 tsp. fresh peeled and minced ginger
3 scallions, cut into 1-1/2-inch lengths
vegetable oil for deep frying

Place mushrooms in small bowl. Cover with water. Let soak at room temperature for 1 hour. Drain. Slice finely and set aside. Marinate chicken in mixture of soy sauce, sherry and sugar for 1 hour. On each square of waxed paper put a heaping tablespoon of a combination of the following ingredients: chicken, ginger, mushrooms and scallions. Fold paper like an envelope, tucking in flap. Put parcels, flap side down, on plate. Heat 2-inches of oil in a deep saucepan to medium-high (375°F.). Fry parcels, 1/2 at a time, for 3 minutes each. Drain. Return all parcels together to hot fat and fry an additional 1-1/2 minutes. Serve immediately. Serves 4 as an appetizer.

ROYAL PEACOCK SILVER WRAPPED CHICKEN

1 chicken breast, skinned and boned
3/4 tsp. salt
1/4 tsp. M.S.G.
1-1/2 tsp. sugar
3 tbs. Hoisin sauce
    (may substitute 4 tbs. catsup)
1/4 tsp. Chinese 5 spice powder
    (substitute mixture of cinnamon and
    ground ginger if 5 spice not available)

1/2 tsp. sesame oil
2 tbs. all-purpose flour
3 tbs. vegetable oil
6 leaves cilantro, minced
1 clove garlic, minced
sixteen 4-inch squares of
    aluminum foil
vegetable oil for frying

Cut breast into 16 pieces. Combine salt, M.S.G., sugar, Hoisin sauce. 5 spice powder, sesame oil, flour, oil, cilantro and garlic. Add chicken, mix well and marinate 2 hours. Wrap each piece of chicken in 4-inch square of foil. Be sure to roll edges of foil twice so juices do not escape. Heat about 2 inches of oil in deep saucepan to medium-high (375°F.). Deep fry each packet 7 minutes. Remove with slotted spoon. Unwrap and serve as appetizer. Makes 4 to 6 appetizer servings.

CHICKEN COOKED WITH FRUIT

Apricot Glazed Chicken............ 138
Chicken with Cherries 139
Chicken in Lemon-Lime Juice....... 140
Chicken in Peach Sauce 141
Grape-Orange Chicken 142
Moroccan Style Lemon Chicken 143
Pineapple Chicken 144
Plum Glazed Chicken 145

APRICOT GLAZED CHICKEN

The ease with which this dish is prepared belies its elegant appearance and rich flavor.

1 cup bottled Russian salad dressing
1/4 cup vegetable oil
1 pkg. (1-3/4 ozs.) dry onion soup mix
1 cup apricot preserves
3 tbs. lemon juice
1 tsp. salt
2 chickens, 3 lbs. each, cut into serving pieces

Mix together salad dressing, oil, soup mix, preserves, lemon juice and salt. Arrange chicken pieces in shallow baking dish. Pour preserve mixture over chicken. Bake for 1 hour at 350°F., or until chicken is tender. Baste twice while baking. Makes 6 to 8 servings.

CHICKEN WITH CHERRIES

A special treat for cherry lovers.

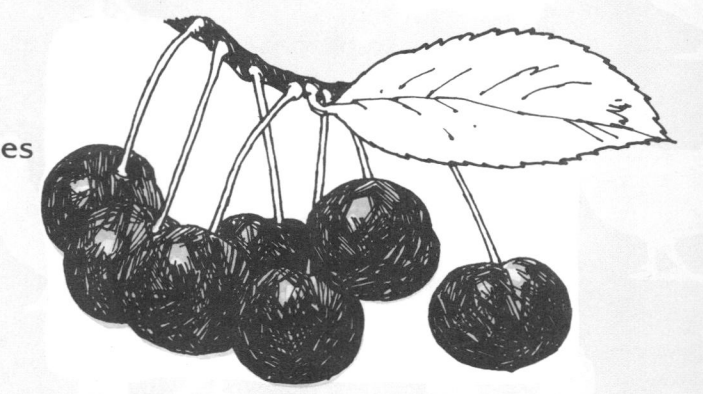

2 cups (17 oz. can) pitted black cherries
1 chicken, 2-1/2 to 3 lbs., cut into serving pieces
salt, paprika and pepper
1/2 cup butter
1 tsp. sugar
1 tbs. flour
dash each of cinnamon and allspice
1 chicken bouillon cube

Drain cherries, reserve syrup. Sprinkle chicken pieces with salt, paprika and pepper. Melt butter over medium-high heat in large skillet. Add chicken to skillet and saute until brown. Remove from skillet and set aside. Add 1/4 teaspoon salt, sugar, flour, cinnamon and allspice to skillet. Gradually stir in cherry syrup. Add chicken and bouillon cube. Cover and bring to a boil. Simmer until chicken is tender, about 40 to 45 minutes. Add cherries during last 5 minutes of cooking time. Makes 4 servings.

CHICKEN IN LEMON-LIME JUICE

An easy to prepare marinade gives this chicken a tropical, tangy flavor. It's best if marinated overnight.

juice of 4 lemons
juice of 4 limes
1 clove garlic, minced
2 tsp. salt
2 tsp. dried tarragon leaves, crushed
1/2 tsp. white pepper
1 cup vegetable oil
1 cup dry white wine
2 chickens, 2-1/2 to 3 lbs. each, cut into serving pieces

Combine lemon and lime juice, garlic, salt, tarragon, pepper, oil and wine in large bowl. Stir to mix. Place chicken pieces in marinade. Cover tightly. Refrigerate at least 8 hours. Turn chicken pieces once while it marinates. Remove chicken from marinade. Place in shallow baking dish. Bake for 1 hour at 375°F., or until done. Baste once with marinade while cooking. Makes 6 to 8 servings.

CHICKEN IN PEACH SAUCE

2 tbs. vegetable oil
1 tsp. salt
1/2 tsp. pepper
1/4 tsp. paprika
1/2 tsp. poultry seasoning
1 chicken, 2-1/2 to 3 lbs.,
    cut into serving pieces

1/4 cup butter
1 cup finely chopped onion
5 tbs. lemon juice
4 large firm fresh peaches
1/2 cup sugar

    Pour oil in large skillet. Place over medium-high heat. Sprinkle chicken with salt, pepper, paprika and poultry seasoning. Place chicken pieces in skillet and saute until brown on all sides. Add 1-1/4 cups water, simmer over low heat 25 minutes. Skim fat and discard. Melt 2 tablespoons butter in another skillet over medium heat and saute onion until golden. Remove onion from skillet. Pour one tablespoon lemon juice over onion and set aside. Wash, peel and slice peaches. Saute peach slices in remaining half of butter until golden. Mix together remaining lemon juice and sugar. Add onion, peaches, juice mixture and 3/4 cup water to chicken. Simmer, covered for 20 minutes. Makes 4 servings.

GRAPE AND ORANGE FLAVORED CHICKEN

3 tbs. flour
1 tsp. salt
1/4 tsp. pepper
1 chicken, 3 lbs., cut into serving pieces
1/3 cup vegetable oil
3 tbs. honey

2 tbs. chopped parsley
3 tbs. grated orange rind
3/4 cup white wine
1/2 cup orange juice
1-1/4 cups seedless grapes

Mix flour, salt and pepper together in a shallow dish. Coat chicken pieces with flour mixture. Pour oil into large skillet. Place over medium-high heat. Add chicken to skillet and saute until brown on all sides. Add honey, parsley, orange rind, wine and juice. Cover and cook 40 minutes longer. Check chicken after it has cooked 20 minutes. If it seems dry, add 1/2-cup water. Remove chicken, skim and discard fat from sauce. Add grapes. Heat, and pour sauce over chicken. Serve immediately. Makes 4 servings.

MOROCCAN STYLE LEMON CHICKEN

1 lemon
1 chicken, 2-1/2 to 3 lbs.
     cut into serving pieces
salt and pepper
2 tbs. butter

2 shallots or scallions, finely chopped
1 clove garlic, minced
3/4 cup chicken stock
1/4 cup chopped fresh parsley
1 tsp. dried oregano

Cut rind of half the lemon into very thin strips. Reserve. Squeeze lemon. Reserve juice. Sprinkle chicken pieces with salt and pepper. Melt butter and oil in skillet over medium-high heat. Saute chicken until brown on all sides. Remove chicken from skillet. Add shallots and garlic to same skillet. Saute until golden. Add 1/4 cup of stock and stir to dissolve all brown particles clinging to bottom of skillet. Cook until liquid is almost evaporated. Add 1/2-cup more of stock. Reduce liquid, over medium heat, to 1/3-cup. Return chicken to skillet, sprinkle with parsley, oregano, lemon rind and juice. Cover and cook slowly, for about 40 minutes, or until chicken is done. Check chicken occasionally. If necessary, add up to 1 cup more chicken broth. Skim and discard fat before serving. Makes 4 servings.

PINEAPPLE CHICKEN

A tart and sweet taste from the Hawaiian Islands.

2 chickens, 2-1/2 to 3 lbs. each, quartered or halved
1/4 cup vegetable oil
salt and pepper
2 tbs. sugar
1 tsp. cornstarch
1 can (8-1/4 ozs.) crushed pineapple
2 tbs. butter or margarine
2 tbs. soy sauce
1 tbs. finely chopped onion

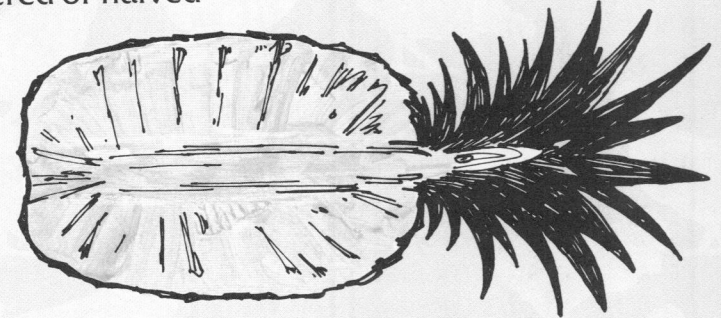

Break joints of chicken. Brush chicken all over with oil. Sprinkle with salt and pepper. Broil or barbecue 4 to 5 inches from heat, 15 to 20 minutes per side. Meanwhile, in small saucepan combine sugar, cornstarch, pineapple, butter, soy sauce and onion. Cook and stir until thickened and bubbly. Spoon mixture over chicken during last 5 minutes of broiling. Makes 6 to 8 servings.

PLUM GLAZED CHICKEN

A savory dish that's plum tasty and extra easy.

1 can (17 ozs.) plums, pitted
1/4 cup frozen orange juice concentrate, thawed
1 tsp. Worcestershire sauce
2 chickens, 2-1/2 to 3 lbs. each, cut into serving pieces
salt and pepper

Dice 3 plums. Set aside. Drain remaining plums, reserving 1-1/2 cups syrup. Combine undiced plums, reserved syrup, orange juice and Worcestershire sauce in blender jar. Blend until smooth. Place chicken pieces in shallow, greased baking dish. Sprinkle chicken with salt and pepper on all sides. Brush all over with plum glaze. Bake at 350°F. for 1 hour, or until chicken is done. Baste chicken with glaze 3 to 4 times during baking process. Skim and discard fat before serving. Add diced plums to remaining glaze. Heat and serve with chicken. Makes 6 to 8 servings.

NUTS AND SEEDS ACCOMPANY CHICKEN

Almond-Encrusted Chicken 148
**Chicken Baked in
 Tomato-Almond Puree** 149
Chicken with Cashews 150
**Chicken with Hazelnuts
 and Buttermilk** 151
Chicken with Walnuts 152
**Chicken with Walnuts and
 Pomegranate Juice** 153
Circassian Chicken. 154
Gallina en Pipian 155

ALMOND-ENCRUSTED CHICKEN

Crunchy almonds add interest to this simple dish. After you roll the chicken in almonds, this dish may be refrigerated for up to 24 hours.

1 egg
1/2 cup milk
1 tsp. salt
1 tsp. paprika
flour
1 chicken, 2-1/2 to 3 lbs., cut into serving pieces
1 cup sliced almonds
1/2 cup vegetable oil

Beat egg lightly with milk, salt and paprika. Dip chicken pieces, one at a time, into flour, then into egg mixture. Roll in almonds. Pour oil into shallow baking dish. Arrange chicken pieces in pan, skin side up. Bake at 375°F. for 1 to 1-1/2 hours, basting twice during baking process. Makes 4 servings.

CHICKEN BAKED IN TOMATO-ALMOND PUREE

1 chicken, 3 lbs.,
   cut into serving pieces
1 cup lime juice
1-1/2 tsp. salt
1 can (17 ozs.) tomatoes, drained
2 whole cloves
6 peppercorns

2 bay leaves
1/4 cup water
2 slices French bread,
   each 1-1/2 inches thick, cubed
1 cup blanched almonds
1/3 cup vegetable oil
tomato and avocado slices (optional)

Marinate chicken pieces in lime juice and 1 teaspoon salt for one hour. Combine tomatoes, cloves, peppercorns, bay leaves, water and 1/2 teaspoon salt in blender jar. Puree. Pour oil in skillet. Place over medium-high heat. Fry bread cubes in oil until golden, about 2 minutes on each side. Drain on paper towels. Add cubes to tomato mixture. Saute almonds in oil until golden. Add almonds to tomato mixture. Puree mixture until smooth. Spread 1/3 of puree mixture in shallow baking dish. Remove chicken from marinade and arrange in dish over puree mixture. Cover with remaining puree. Bake uncovered, at 350°F. until chicken is tender, about 45 minutes. Garnish with tomato and avocado slices, if desired. Makes 4 servings.

CHICKEN WITH CASHEW NUTS

The flavors of chicken and cashew nuts harmonize especially well in this dish.

1 egg white
2 chicken breasts, skinned, boned and diced
1/2 tsp. salt
1-1/2 tsp. soy sauce
2 tsp. sherry
1/2 tsp. sugar
1/2 tsp. sesame oil
2 tsp. cornstarch
3 tbs. vegetable oil
3/4 cup salted cashews

Beat egg white in large bowl until foamy. Add chicken, salt, soy sauce, sherry, sugar, sesame oil and cornstarch to egg white. Pour oil in wok or large skillet. Place over high heat. Stir fry about 2 minutes. Add cashews, mix well, and serve immediately. Makes 4 servings.

CHICKEN WITH HAZELNUTS AND BUTTERMILK

A blender or food processor will make quick work of the hazelnuts.

1/4 cup butter, melted
6 ozs. hazelnuts, ground
1 tsp. salt
1 tsp. pepper

1-1/2 cups buttermilk
1 chicken, 3 lbs., cut into serving pieces
3 tbs. flour
1 cup milk

Pour butter into 13 x 9 x 2-inch baking dish. Combine hazelnuts, salt and pepper in deep bowl. Pour buttermilk into another deep bowl. Dip chicken pieces in buttermilk. Roll in nut mixture. Reserve 1 cup buttermilk for gravy. Roll each chicken piece in baking dish. Place chicken, skin side up, in dish (pieces should not touch each other). Bake 1 hour and 15 minutes at 350°F. Baste every 15 to 20 minutes. Remove chicken to serving platter and keep warm in 200°F. oven while you make gravy. To make gravy, pour 3 to 4 tablespoons of chicken drippings into saucepan. Spoon any nuts remaining in baking dish into saucepan. Add flour and simmer over medium heat for 3 to 4 minutes, stirring. Stir in milk and reserved buttermilk. Increase heat and bring to boil. Pour sauce over chicken and serve. Makes 4 servings.

CHICKEN WITH WALNUTS

A quickly prepared chicken dish with lots of vegetables and nuts. Serve it with rice and a Mandarin orange salad.

2 tbs. cornstarch
1 tsp. sugar
1 tbs. soy sauce
1/4 cup vegetable oil
1/2 cup coarsely chopped walnuts
1 onion, sliced

1 sweet red pepper, seeded, deribbed and sliced
2 cups diced cooked chicken
1-1/2 cups chicken broth
2 tbs. sherry
3/4 cup chopped celery

Mix together cornstarch, sugar and soy sauce to make a smooth paste. Pour oil into wok or large skillet. Place over high heat. Saute walnuts, onion and pepper in oil 4 to 5 minutes. Add chicken and chicken broth. Stir. Blend in cornstarch paste and simmer 3 to 5 minutes, stirring constantly. Add sherry and celery and cook 2 minutes more. Serve immediately. Makes 4 servings.

CHICKEN WITH WALNUTS AND POMEGRANATE JUICE

3 tbs. olive oil
1 onion, thickly sliced
1/2 tsp. turmeric
1 cup ground walnuts
3-3/4 cups chicken stock
salt and pepper

1 chicken **OR** duck, 3-1/2 to 4 lbs.,
    cut into serving pieces
juice of 1 lemon
1/3 cup pomegranate juice
1/2 cup sugar
rice to serve 4

Pour olive oil into a large skillet. Place over medium-high heat. Fry onion with turmeric until golden brown, about 10 minutes. Remove onion from skillet and place in saucepan. Add ground walnuts and chicken stock to saucepan. Season mixture with salt and pepper. Bring to boil. Cover and simmer, stirring occasionally for 20 minutes. In original skillet, saute chicken pieces until brown. Transfer to 13 x 9 x 2-inch baking dish. Pour walnut sauce over chicken. Cover and bake at 350°F. for 30 minutes. Skim fat and discard. Mix lemon juice, pomegranate juice and sugar together. Pour over chicken and walnut sauce. Stir well. Cover and bake for 30 minutes. Arrange chicken on platter of rice. Cover with sauce. Makes 4 servings.

CIRCASSIAN CHICKEN

A famous chicken dish from Turkey which has a rich walnut-thickened sauce.

3 whole cloves
3 onions
1 chicken, 2-1/2 to 3 lbs., cut into serving pieces
3 stalks celery
1 bay leaf
1-1/2 tsp. salt

8 peppercorns
1-1/2 cups walnuts
1/2 cup soft bread crumbs
1 to 2 tbs. paprika
1/4 tsp. cayenne pepper

Boil 2 quarts water in Dutch oven or large saucepan. Stick a clove into each onion. Add chicken, onions, celery, bay leaf, salt and peppercorns to water. Simmer 1 to 1-1/2 hours, or until chicken is tender. Remove chicken. By boiling, uncovered, reduce stock to one half its original volume. Strain and cool to lukewarm. Puree walnuts in blender jar. Add bread crumbs, 2 tablespoons reduced stock, paprika and cayenne. Blend again. Slowly add about 2 cups of lukewarm stock. Blend briefly until mixture has consistency of thin mayonnaise. Skin and bone chicken. Cut meat into bite-sized pieces. Spoon sauce over chicken and serve. Makes 4 servings.

GALLINA EN PIPIAN

This thick, nut sauce is marvelous on chicken. For a change, combine sauce and chicken and spoon mixture into hot, flour tortillas. You may use leftover, cooked chicken in this recipe too.

1 large chicken, cut into serving pieces, or 2 cups cubed cooked chicken
salt and pepper
5 cups chicken broth
1 can (6 ozs.) green chilies, seeded
1/2 cup **EACH** toasted pumpkin seeds and corn nuts
1/2 cup peanuts
2 cloves garlic, peeled
1 tsp. **EACH** salt and pepper

Boil 1-1/2 quarts of water in large saucepan or Dutch oven. Add chicken, salt and pepper. Simmer for 1 hour, or until chicken is tender. Remove chicken from saucepan. Reserve broth. When chicken is cool, remove meat from bones and cut into small pieces. Combine chilies with 1 cup reserved chicken broth, corn nuts, pumpkin seeds, peanuts and garlic in a blender jar. Blend until smooth. Add remaining chicken broth to sauce. Cook 10 minutes, stirring occasionally. Spoon sauce over cooked chicken. Makes 4 to 6 servings.

PRECOOKED AND LEFTOVER CHICKEN

Chicken Croquettes.............. 158
Chicken Divan 159
Chicken-Dressing Bake 160
Chicken au Gratin 161
Chicken Praline Crepes 164
Chicken and
   Tangerine Stuffed Crepes...... 162
Chicken in Toast Cups........... 165
Chicken Tetrazinni.............. 166
Chicken-Zucchini Casserole 167
Curried Chicken Puff 168
Savory Chicken Salad 169

CHICKEN CROQUETTES

3 tbs. melted butter
1/4 cup all-purpose flour
1/2 cup milk
1/2 cup chicken broth
1 tbs. chopped fresh parsley
1 tsp. lemon juice
1 tsp. finely chopped onion

1/2 tsp. salt
dash **EACH** pepper, nutmeg, paprika
1-1/2 cups cooked chicken
1 beaten egg
2 tbs. water
3/4 cup fine dry bread crumbs
vegetable oil for deep frying

Melt butter in skillet over medium heat. Add flour. Cook until mixture bubbles for 30 seconds, while stirring constantly. Stir in milk and broth. Cook, stirring until mixture thickens. Cook 1 minute. Add parsley, lemon juice, onion, salt, pepper, nutmeg and paprika. Remove from heat. Cool. Add chicken. Chill thoroughly. Mix egg and water in small bowl. With wet hands shape chicken mixture into 8 balls. Roll balls in bread crumbs, then egg-water mixture, then crumbs again. Heat about 2-inches of oil in a heavy skillet. Fry croquettes 2-1/2 to 3 minutes. Drain on paper towels. Makes 4 servings.

CHICKEN DIVAN

A classic favorite that combines broccoli and chicken in a creamy, cheese sauce.

2 pkgs. (10 ozs. each) frozen broccoli
1 can (10-3/4 ozs.) cream of chicken soup
1 tbs. lemon juice
1 tsp. Worcestershire sauce
1/4 tsp. nutmeg

1/2 cup grated Parmesan cheese
2 cups chopped cooked chicken
1/2 cup whipping cream
1/2 cup mayonnaise
1 tsp. paprika

Cook broccoli according to package directions. Drain well. Arrange in greased shallow baking dish. Mix soup, lemon juice, Worcestershire and nutmeg together well in a bowl. Pour 1/2 of this mixture over broccoli. Sprinkle with 2 tablespoons Parmeasan cheese. Add chicken and pour remaining soup mixture over all. Bake, uncovered 30 minutes at 300°F. Whip cream and fold in mayonnaise. Spread over chicken. Top with remaining cheese and paprika. Broil for 2 minutes about 4 inches from heat, until golden. Makes 4 to 6 servings.

CHICKEN-DRESSING BAKE

You don't have to go to the trouble of preparing stuffed roast chicken to enjoy chicken and dressing. Try this easy and colorful dish.

1 pkg. (8 ozs.) herb-seasoned stuffing mix
1 can (10-1/2 ozs.) cream of mushroom soup
2 cups chicken stock
2 well-beaten eggs
2-1/2 cups diced, cooked chicken
1/2 cup milk
2 tbs. chopped canned pimiento

Toss stuffing mix with 1/2 can of soup, 2 cups stock and eggs. Spread mixture in shallow baking dish. Top with chicken. Mix together milk, pimiento and remaining soup. Pour over chicken-dressing mixture. Cover with foil. Bake at 350°F. for 45 minutes. Makes 4 to 6 servings.

CHICKEN AU GRATIN

Serve with crusty French bread and a fresh green salad.

1/4 cup butter or margarine
1/4 cup all-purpose flour
1 tsp. salt
1/2 tsp. pepper
2 cups milk
1/2 cup shredded sharp Cheddar cheese
4 cups chopped cooked chicken
1/2 cup bread crumbs

Melt butter in large skillet over medium heat. Add flour, salt and pepper. Cook, stirring constantly, for about 7 to 8 minutes. Gradually add milk. Cook, stirring constantly until sauce is thick and smooth. Add cheese. Continue cooking and stirring until melted. Remove skillet from heat. Place chicken in buttered casserole and pour cheese sauce on top. Sprinkle with bread crumbs. Bake at 350°F. for 35 to 40 minutes. Makes 4 to 6 servings.

CHICKEN-TANGERINE STUFFED CREPES

The next two recipes present delicious ways to prepare leftover chicken in crepes. An easy and foolproof recipe for crepes precedes the filling recipes.

CREPES

6 tbs. butter	1/4 cup milk	1 tbs. brandy (optional)
2 eggs	1/4 cup water	1/2 cup all-purpose flour
		1/2 tsp. salt

Have ready a small frying pan or skillet (bottom measurement of 6 to 8 inches) or crepe pan, a blender or electric beater, small spatula and a warm plate. In skillet, melt butter until foaming over medium heat. Skim and discard foam. Carefully pour out clear amber liquid butter, discarding milky residue. This is called "clarified" butter. Use clarified butter in recipe and for cooking crepes. Combine eggs, milk, water, brandy, 1 tablespoon clarified butter, flour and salt in blender jar. Blend until smooth. Let batter stand at room temperature 1 hour. When ready to cook, heat small skillet until quite hot. Add 1/2 teaspoon clarified butter and about 2 tablespoons batter. Rotate pan so a thin film of batter forms on bottom. Work quickly, crepe will be ready to turn in 15 to 20 seconds. When crepe has browned on one side, use spatula to flip over. Let opposite side cook 15 seconds. Slide onto warmed plate. Repeat procedure, buttering pan before each crepe. Makes 12 to 16 crepes.

CHICKEN TANGERINE STUFFING

1 can (6 ozs.) water chestnuts, drained and sliced
1 can (8 ozs.) tangerines, drained
2 cups diced, cooked chicken
1/2 cup **EACH** mayonnaise and chopped almonds
2 tbs. sherry

1/2 tsp. salt
SAUCE
1/2 cup mayonnaise
1/2 cup sour cream

Combine water chestnuts, tangerines, chicken, mayonnaise, almonds, sherry and salt. Mix gently, but thoroughly. Place 2 tablespoons mixture on each crepe and fold sides together. Place rolled crepes into greased baking dish. Combine all sauce ingredients. Pour over crepes. Bake at 325°F. for 30 minutes. Makes 4 to 6 servings.

CHICKEN PRALINE CREPES

A rich, prize winning recipe. Use the crepe recipe on page 162.

CREPE FILLING
2 cups diced, cooked chicken
3/4 cup slivered almonds
3/4 cup halved pecans
1 tbs. minced watercress
1/2 cup sour cream
1/2 tsp. **EACH** salt and white pepper
12 crepes (see recipe, page 162)

BRANDIED CHERRY SAUCE
1 can (9-1/2 ozs.) dark, sweet cherries, pitted
1/4 cup firmly packed brown sugar
1/2 cup apricot brandy
2 tbs. cornstarch

Mix together chicken, almonds, pecans, watercress, sour cream, salt and pepper. Spoon filling into crepes, fold sides together. Line bottom of greased shallow baking dish with folded crepes. Bake at 300°F. for 20 minutes. Prepare sauce. Heat cherries and syrup in small saucepan 5 minutes. Add sugar and brandy. Stir until sugar dissolves. Add cornstarch and cook until thickened. Pour sauce over cooked crepes. Makes 4 to 6 servings.

CHICKEN IN TOAST CUPS

An interesting appetizer that can be prepared in a jiffy.

3/4 cup diced, cooked chicken
1/4 cup finely chopped celery
1/4 cup finely chopped onion
1/2 cup seedless grapes, halved (optional)
1/2 cup mayonnaise
1/2 tsp. salt
1/4 tsp. pepper
12 slices white bread
1/4 cup melted butter

Mix together chicken, celery, onion, grapes, mayonniase, salt and pepper. Cut out 24 2-inch rounds of bread. Brush both sides with melted butter and press into 1 3/4-inch muffin tin cups. Bake bread rounds at 350°F. for 10 to 12 minutes, or until golden brown. Remove from oven and cool. Fill each cup with 1-1/2 teaspoons chicken mixture and serve. Makes 4 servings.

CHICKEN TETRAZINNI

This dish was invented in honor of an opera star, and bears her name.

1/4 cup butter
3/4 lb. mushrooms, sliced
1 green pepper, slivered
3 tbs. all-purpose flour
1-1/2 tsp. salt
1/4 tsp. pepper
2-1/2 cups half and half (light cream)

4 cups diced, cooked chicken
1/4 cup sherry
1/4 tsp. Tabasco sauce
6 ozs. uncooked spaghetti
2 egg yolks, beaten
2 tbs. grated Parmesan cheese

Melt butter in skillet over medium heat. Saute mushrooms and pepper 5 minutes. Blend in flour, salt and pepper. Add cream, stirring constantly. Cook until thickened. Add chicken and sherry, and heat. Season with Tabasco sauce. Cook spaghetti according to package directions. Drain spaghetti and pour into shallow greased baking dish. Add small amount of chicken mixture to egg yolks, then stir yolks into remaining chicken mixture. Pour over spaghetti. Sprinkle with cheese. Bake at 300°F. for 45 minutes. Makes 6 servings.

CHICKEN-ZUCCHINI CASSEROLE

4 ozs. Italian sausage
4 medium zucchini (1-1/2 lbs.)
1/2 cup grated Parmesan cheese
1/2 cup fine bread crumbs
1-1/2 cups diced, cooked chicken
1 tbs. chopped, fresh parsley

1/2 tsp. salt
1/4 tsp. pepper
3 eggs, separated
1/4 cup milk
1 tbs. butter, melted
1/2 tsp. paprika

Brown sausage in skillet. Drain fat and discard. In small amount of water cook whole zucchini. When just tender, chop finely. Combine cheese and crumbs in large bowl. Set aside 2 tablespoons of cheese-crumb mixture. Add chicken, parsley, salt, pepper and chopped zucchini to cheese-crumb mixture in large bowl. Beat egg whites until stiff. In a separate bowl, beat together yolks and milk. Stir into chicken mixture. Gently fold in egg whites. Turn into greased shallow baking dish. Sprinkle with reserved crumbs mixed with melted butter and paprika. Bake uncovered at 325°F. for 35 to 40 minutes. Makes 4 to 6 servings.

CURRIED CHICKEN PUFF

This subtly flavored dish is a snap to prepare. The curry also lends a delicate yellow color.

1 can (10 ozs.) cream of chicken soup
2 cups cooked, finely diced chicken
2 tsp. curry powder
4 egg yolks, beaten
1/4 cup chopped, fresh parsley
4 stiffly beaten egg whites
2 tbs. grated coconut

Combine soup, chicken and curry powder in skillet over medium heat. Heat thoroughly. Remove from heat and stir mixture slowly into beaten egg yolks. Fold mixture and chopped parsley into egg whites. Pour into greased casserole dish or souffle dish. Sprinkle with coconut. Set in pan of hot water. Bake at 350°F. for 35 to 45 minutes. Insert knife into center. When done, knife should come out clean. Serve at once. Makes 4 servings.

SAVORY CHICKEN SALAD

Great served on a bed of lettuce or in a sandwich. For variety serve it in a tomato or avocado shell.

2 cups diced, cooked chicken
1 cup diced celery
1/2 tsp. salt
1/4 tsp. pepper
1/2 cup mayonnaise or salad dressing (Green Goddess is good)
lettuce leaves
wedges of hard-cooked eggs, pickles, pickled beets, radishes, tomato wedges, sliced cucumber and olives for garnish (all optional)
1/2 cup slivered almonds

Mix together chicken, celery, salt, pepper and mayonnaise. Serve on salad greens, adding optional ingredients as garnishes.

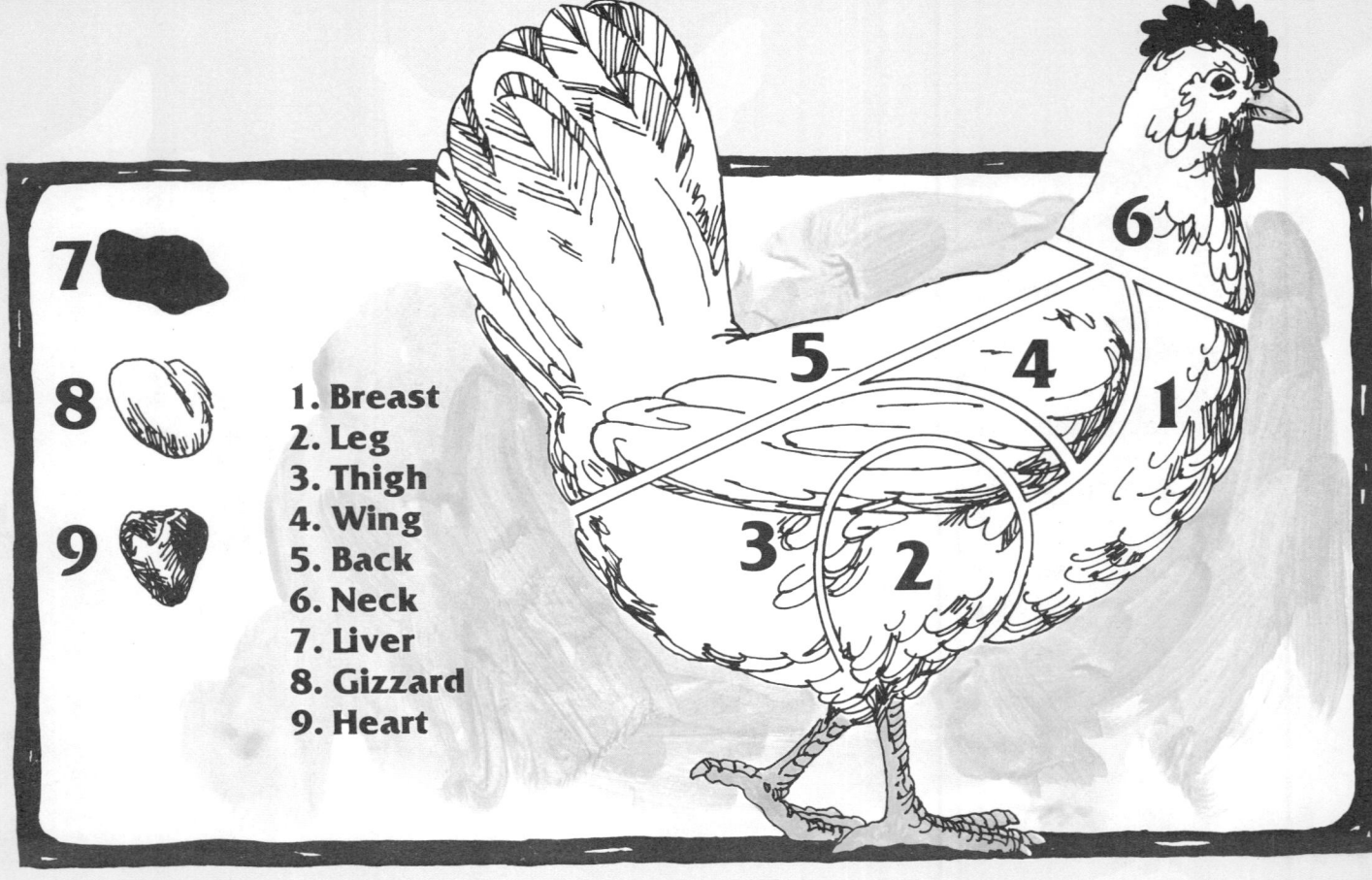

CHICKEN PARTS

Chicken Gizzards, Sauce Pietro 173
Chicken Hearts in Sour Cream 174
Chicken Livers in Port Wine 176
Chicken Wings Parmesan 177
Rumaki 172
Spicy Chinese Chicken Wings 175

RUMAKI

A sophisticated Island favorite that is a popular appetizer on the Mainland as well.

1 doz. large chicken livers, intact
1 can (6 ozs.) drained water chestnuts
12 slices smoked bacon
1 cup soy sauce
6 tsp. dry sherry
2 cloves garlic, minced
1/2 tsp. ginger juice or minced fresh ginger

Cut the livers in half. Wrap liver around a whole water chestnut (or half of large one). Wrap 1/2-slice bacon around both, and skewer with toothpick. Make marinade of soy sauce, sherry, garlic, and ginger. Marinate skewered livers 1 to 4 hours in the refrigerator, turning once or twice. Drain. Broil until bacon is nearly crisp, turning once. Makes 6 to 8 appetizer servings.

CHICKEN GIZZARDS, SAUCE PIETRO

1/4 lb. bacon, finely chopped
1 tbs. olive oil
1 small onion, minced
2 garlic cloves, minced
1 lb. chicken gizzards, chopped
2 parsley sprigs, minced
1/4 to 1/2 tsp. crushed red pepper
1/4 tsp. ground cloves

1/2 tsp. crumbled dried marjoram
1/2 tsp. salt
1 cup dry red wine
2 cups fresh or canned, chopped tomatoes
2 cans (6 ozs. each) tomato paste
4 cups water
8 ozs. thin spaghetti
grated Romano or Parmesan cheese

Cook bacon, olive oil, onion and garlic in large saucepan over medium heat until bacon is nearly crisp. Add gizzards, parsley, red pepper, cloves, marjoram and salt. Cook 2 to 3 minutes. Add wine. Simmer, covered for about 25 minutes. Add tomatoes, tomato paste and water. Simmer until fairly thick. Cook spaghetti according to package directions and drain. Sprinkle platter with cheese. Add spaghetti to platter, cover with sauce and sprinkle with more cheese. Makes 6 servings.

CHICKEN HEARTS IN SOUR CREAM

An unusual but delightful recipe for those who fancy variety-type meats.

4 tbs. butter
1 lb. chicken hearts, split
1/2 onion, chopped
1 clove garlic, minced
1/2 lb. fresh mushrooms, halved
1/4 cup dry white wine
1 tsp. salt

1/4 tsp. pepper
1/4 tsp. basil
1/4 tsp. oregano
1/4 tsp. thyme
3/4 cup cream of celery **OR** cream of chicken soup
1/3 cup sour cream

Melt 2 tablespoons butter in skillet over medium heat. Saute chicken hearts, onions and garlic for 10 minutes. Add remaining 2 tablespoons butter and mushrooms. Saute 5 minutes. Add wine, salt, pepper, basil, oregano and thyme. Simmer 20 to 25 minutes, until hearts are tender. Mix soup and sour cream together. Add to stew. Heat and serve. Makes 4 servings.

SPICY CHINESE CHICKEN WINGS

Hoisin sauce has a sweet and pungent flavor. It's available in the Oriental sections of most supermarkets.

1/4 cup sesame oil
1/2 cup soy sauce
1/4 cup honey
2 green onions, chopped
1 tsp. garlic powder
3 tbs. Hoisin sauce
2 to 3 lbs. chicken wings (tips removed and discarded), cut into 2 pieces each

Mix sesame oil, soy sauce, honey, onions, garlic powder and Hoisin sauce together in a shallow glass dish. Add wings and marinate 4 to 6 hours in the refrigerator. Place in shallow baking dish and bake at 350°F. for 30 minutes. Remove from oven and cool. Just before serving broil 5 minutes to brown. Watch carefully during broiling to keep wings from charing. Makes 6 to 8 appetizer servings

CHICKEN LIVERS IN PORT WINE

A savory favorite, equally suited for chafing dish or stove top cooking.

1/3 cup butter or margarine
4 green onions, finely chopped
1 lb. chicken livers
1/4 tsp. dried sage
1/2 tsp. salt
2 tbs. lemon juice
2/3 cup Port wine
1/4 tsp. freshly ground pepper
slices of toast

Melt butter in skillet over medium heat. Saute onions in butter for 8 to 10 minutes. Add livers, saute 4 minutes. Stir in sage, salt, lemon juice, Port and pepper. Simmer about 8 minutes, stirring occasionally. Correct seasonings and serve on toast. Makes 3 to 4 servings.

CHICKEN WINGS, PARMESAN

Chicken wings have become fashionable and popular as appetizers.

2 to 2-1/2 lbs. chicken wings
1/3 cup butter or margarine, melted
2/3 cup all-purpose flour
1-1/2 tsp. salt
1/3 cup grated Parmesan cheese
1/2 tsp. paprika
1/2 tsp. oregano
1/2 cup buttermilk

Cut off tips of wings. Discard or save in freezer for chicken broth. Pour butter into foil-lined shallow baking dish. Preheat oven to 400°F. Mix flour, salt, cheese, paprika, and oregano together in a bowl. Dip wings in buttermilk, roll in flour-cheese mixture, then in melted butter. Bake in foil-lined dish 1 hour, or until crisp. Makes 4 servings as main dish, or 6 to 8 servings as appetizer.

INDEX

a la Normande 88
Almond
   Almond-Encrusted 148
   Almond Chicken Casserole 54
   Tomato-Almond Puree 149
Amarentto 97
Apricot Glazed 138
Au Gratin 161
Barbecued
   Introduction 44
   Caraway Chicken Halves 46
   Teriyaki 47
   Foil-Wrapped 51
   Grilled Island 48
   Sweet and Sour 49
   Texas 50
Basic
   Breast Cutlets 86
   Stew 80
   Stir-Fried 128
Boning, How to 12
Bouillon 71
Braising 6

Breasts
   Basic Breast Cutlets 86
   Sesame Cutlets 87
   a la Normande 88
   Picatta 89
   In Rum Crumbs 90
   Savoyarde 92
   Veronique 91
Broiling Techniques 44
Broth 71
Burgundy (Coq Au Vin) 98
Butters, Flavored 34
Cacciatore 74
Calabrian (stew) 76
Calvados 99
Caraway 46
Carving, How to 30
Cashews 150
Casseroles
   Almond 54
   Hacienda 55
   Sauerkraut 56
   Sweet Potato Pie 57
   Vegetable 58

Creamy Baked. 59
   Popover Tarragon. 60
   Easy Pot Pie. 61
Cherries 139
Chinese Lemon. 132
Chinese Spicy Wings 175
Chowder, Corn and Chicken 65
Circassian. 154
Cock-a-Leekie Soup 70
Consomme 64
Coq Au Vin (Burgundy) 98
Corn Chowder 65
Corsican (stew) 78
Cranberry Orange Stuffing 38
Cream and Calvados 99
Cream, Wine and Mushrooms 100
Creamy Baked 59
Crepes
   Praline 164
   Tangerine Stuffed. 162
Croquettes 158
Cucumber Soup 66
Cups, Toast. 165
Curried, Puff 168

Curry. 108
Cutlets
   Basic Breast. 86
   Sesame 87
Deep Fried. 124
Disjointing Chicken 9
Divan. 159
Dressing Bake 160
Dumplings, Chicken and 80
Easy Pot Pie. 61
Flavored Butters. 34
Foil-Wrapped (BBQ) 51
Freezing, How to. 6
Fried
   Chicken Stew 82
   Maryland. 125
   Deep Fried. 124
   Stir-Fried 128
Fruits
   Apricot Glazed 138
   Cherries. 139
   Lemon-Lime Juice 140
   Peach Sauce 141
   Grape-Orange 142

Moroccan Style. 143
  Pineapple 144
  Plum Glazed 145
Gallina en Pipian 155
Garlic 112
Giblet Soup. 67
Ginger and Anise. 111
Gizzards
  Sauce Pietro 173
  Grape-Orange 142
  Grilled Island 48
  Gumbo Soup. 68
  Hacienda. 55
  Ham Marsala 102
  Hazelnuts with Buttermilk 151
  Hearts in Sour Cream. 174
  Homemade Broth or Bouillon 71
International Classics
  Kiev 118
  Mole 120
  Maryland Fried 125
  Paella Valenciana 122
  Deep Fried. 124
  Tandoori 119
Kiev. 118
Leftover and Precooked (see Precooked)157
Lemon. 132
Lemon-Lime 140
Livers in Port Wine. 176
Marinating, About 20
Maryland Fried 125
Master Recipes, roasting
  Stuffed. 36
  Unstuffed 32
Mole 120
Moroccan Style 143
Mustard Surprise. 114
New Brunswick Stew 83
Nuts and Seeds
  Almond-Encrusted. 148
  Baked in Tomato-Almond Puree . . 149
  Cashews 150
  Hazelnuts and Buttermilk 151
  Walnuts. 152
  Walnuts and Pomegranate Juice. . . 153
  Circassian 154
  Gallina en Pipian. 155
Nutritive Value 8

Orange Cranberry Stuffing 38
Orange Rum Baked 96
Oriental Delicacies
   Basic Stir-Fried 128
   Sauteed with Hoisin Sauce and
      Green Peppers 129
   Velvet and Peas 130
   Lemon 132
   Paper Wrapped 134
   Royal Peacock Silver Wrapped 135
   Simmered Japanese 131
Paella Vallenciana 122
Paper Wrapped 134
Paprika (stew) 77
Parmesan Wings 177
Parts
   Gizzards, Sauce Pietro 173
   Hearts in Sour Cream 174
   Livers in Port Wine 176
   Wings, Parmesan 177
   Rumaki 172
   Spicy Chinese Wings 175
Peach Sauce 141
Picatta (breasts) 89

Pie, Easy Pot 61
Pie, Sweet Potato 57
Pineapple 144
Plum Glazed 145
Popover Tarragon 60
Pot Pie, Easy 61
Praline Crepes 164
Precooked and Leftover
   Croquettes 158
   Divan 159
   Dressing Bake 160
   au Gratin 161
   Praline Crepes 164
   Tangerine Stuffed Crepes 162
   Toast Cups 165
   Tetrazinni 166
   Zucchini Casserole 167
   Curried Puff 168
   Savory Salad 169
Roast
   Introduction 24
   Roasting Timetable 26
   How to Truss a Chicken 28
   How to Carve a Roast Chicken 30

Master Recipe, unstuffed............ 32
Flavored Butters.................. 34
Master Recipe, Stuffed............ 36
Stuffings
Simple Grape 37
Simple Bread................... 37
Bread, Nut and Apple............ 37
Cranberry-Orange............... 38
Brandied-Pecan................. 39
Spit-Roasted....................... 40
Roasted in Salt.................... 41
Royal Peacock Silver Wrapped....... 135
Rum Crumbs (breast)................ 90
Rumaki........................... 172
Sake Sauce........................ 103
Salad, Savory...................... 169
Sauerkraut (casserole).............. 56
Sauteed with Hoisin and Green Peppers 129
Sauteeing......................... 16
Savory Salad...................... 169
Savoryarde (breasts)............... 92
Senegalese Soup................... 69
Sesame Cutlets.................... 87
Simmered in Beer.................. 104

Simmered Japanese................. 131
Simple Bread Stuffing.............. 37
Simple Grape Stuffing.............. 37
Soups
Consume....................... 64
Corn Chowder.................. 65
Cucumber...................... 66
Giblet......................... 67
Gumbo........................ 68
Senegalese.................... 69
Cock-a-Leekie................. 70
Homemade Broth or Bouillon..... 71
Sour Cream Baked.................. 115
Sour Cream Hearts................. 174
Spices
Curry......................... 108
Vinegar Sauce.................. 110
Garlic........................ 112
Ginger and Anise............... 111
Mustard Surprise............... 114
Sour Cream Baked............... 115
Spicy Chinese Wings............ 175
Spirited in Clay.................... 105
Spit Roasted...................... 40

Stews
    Caciatore...........................74
    Calabrian..........................76
    Paprika............................77
    Corsican Style.....................78
    With Dumplings....................80
    Chickpea-Lemon...................79
    Fried..............................82
    New Brunswick....................83
Stir-Fried.............................128
Stuffing
    Brandied Pecan....................39
    Bread, Nut and Apple..............37
    Cranberry-Orange.................38
    Simple Bread......................37
    Simple Grape......................37
Sweet and Sour (BBQ).................49
Sweet Potato (casserole)...............57
Tandoori.............................119
Tangerine Stuffed Crepes.............162
Teriyaki...............................47
Tetrazinni...........................166
Texas (BBQ)..........................50
Timetable, Roasting...................26

Toast Cups..........................165
Truss, How to........................28
Velvet and Peas.....................130
Veronique............................91
Vegetable Casserole..................58
Vinegar Sauce, chicken with.........110
Walnuts.............................152
Walnuts with Pomegranate Juice......153
Wine and Spirits
    Baked Orange-Rum.................96
    Amaretto..........................97
    Cooked in Burgundy Wine..........98
    Cream and Calvados...............99
    Cream, Wine and Mushrooms......100
    Ham Marsala......................102
    Sake Sauce.......................103
    Simmered in Beer.................104
    Spirited in Clay..................105
Wings, Parmesan.....................177
Wings, Spicy Chinese.................175
Wrapped, Paper......................134
Wrapped Silver.......................135
Zucchini Casserole...................167